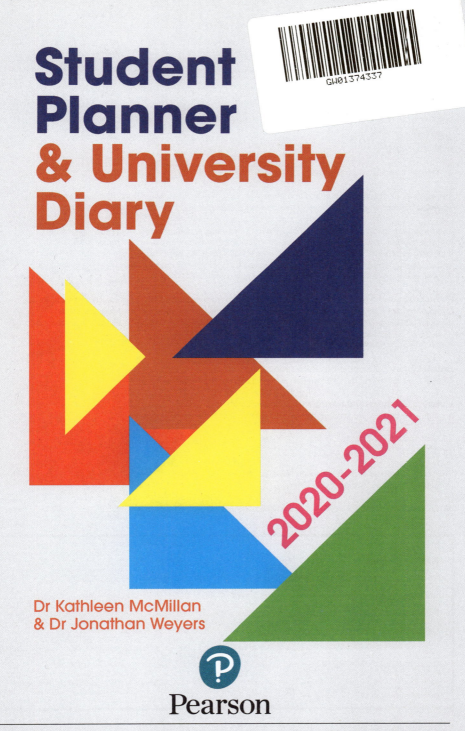

Student Planner & University Diary

2020-2021

Dr Kathleen McMillan
& Dr Jonathan Weyers

Pearson

Harlow, England • London • New York • Boston • San Francisco • Toronto • Sydney • Dubai • Singapore • Hong Kong
Tokyo • Seoul • Taipei • New Delhi • Cape Town • São Paulo • Mexico City • Madrid • Amsterdam • Munich • Paris • Milan

PEARSON EDUCATION LIMITED
KAO Two
KAO Park
Harlow, CM17 9SR
United Kingdom
Tel: +44 (0)1279 623623
Web: www.pearson.com/uk

Published 2020

Public holidays and notable dates have been obtained from published UK sources where possible. Dates of religious festivals have been derived from a variety of international sources and are as accurate as it is possible to be when there are often differences in observation dates across the world.

ISBN: 978-1-292-33270-3 (print)

British Library Cataloguing-in-Publication Data
A catalogue record for the print edition is available from the British Library

Library of Congress Cataloging-in-Publication Data
A catalog record for the print edition is available from the Library of Congress

10 9 8 7 6 5 4 3 2 1
24 23 22 21 20

Print edition typeset in 9/12 Helvetica Neue LT W1G by SPi Global
Print edition printed and bound in China.

NOTE THAT ANY PAGE CROSS REFERENCES REFER TO THE PRINT EDITION

This book belongs to:	
If found, please contact:	
Mobile number:	
Email address:	

For emergency contacts, see p 14

Contents

Why plan?

Effective planning and scheduling will help you to be organised and manage your time more effectively. These are life skills that will make you efficient and help you achieve more in your life. As a student, you are expected to do this on your own without the help of mentors, teachers or parents. You can use this planner to make a difference as you learn independently at university. Relevant strands of planning activity include the following:

- **Personal planning**. This is all about time management, keeping your social life and employment commitments in order and helping you to remember key dates and events.
- **Planning for your studies**. At university you will be given a range of assignments, some very complex, and be expected to deliver these on time. Planning can help you spread the workload, take account of social and employment commitments and produce a higher quality outcome.
- **Planning for exams**. Organisation and time management are most important when studying for exams. You'll need to allocate time across your subjects for adequate revision, taking into account your other commitments. Doing this effectively will help you cope with exam stress.
- **Financial planning**. Often overlooked, keeping control of your cash can be an issue for many students. It is all too easy to miscalculate university costs. A financial budget can help you to plan your expenditure more evenly and take account of predictable 'blips' in spending.
- **Longer-term planning**. For your future career, you'll want to develop as a person and as a student; this means paying attention to the longer term. For example, by taking account of the feedback from your tutors and reflecting on the reasons why you achieved particular grades, you can plan for and produce better work in the future. This may feed into a personal development plan, or similar, as promoted by most universities.

How to plan and schedule effectively

This *Student Planner & University Diary 2020–21* has been designed to help you to note the events, meetings, deadlines and 'to do' lists that make up student life. It will also provide you with practical and timely help and advice for planning, studying and managing your time. Its features include:

Semester/term planner and timetable

Easy-to-reference planner for each study period of the academic year, ensuring that you know where you need to be and when.

Monthly planner and 'to do' lists

A handy overview of any key events and reminders throughout the month, enabling you to plan ahead and remember those important assignment deadlines, labs and tutorials, as well as birthdays and social events.

Monthly learning ideas and reminders

A series of prompts that follow the rhythm of the academic year that will help you to be organised and keep up with the work as you progress through the terms/semesters.

Weekly study skill and strategy tips

Tips that relate to developing your study skills and organised around the different strands of your university life. These will help you to be proactive and effective in your learning activities by anticipating tasks ahead of time. They will help you to produce work that meets high standards and to reflect on what you have achieved.

Week-to-view academic diary

Designed to help you to organise your week.

Planning resources section

The skills tips throughout the diary are supported by and cross-referenced to a comprehensive planning resources section (pages 185–270 at the end of the diary section). This includes many checklists, outline planning tables, practical reference information and advice for specific activities, and will be invaluable in referencing and reinforcing your academic skills. It also includes essential features such as a personal budget planner and revision timetables. 'To do' lists will help you prioritise and complete tasks. These pages are copyright-free and may be photocopied for personal use.

The Study Skills Book

All of the skills, tips and planning resources are based on the authors' successful study skills handbook, *The Study Skills Book* (3rd edition), which contains 71 chapters covering these and other aspects of student life in much more detail and is an invaluable resource to help make the most out of your studies and your time at university (see page 266 of this book for details). We hope you find your *Student Planner & University Diary* useful and would be extremely grateful for any suggestions for additions you might like to make.

Dr Kathleen McMillan and Dr Jonathan Weyers

Calendar 2020-21

July 2020

Mon	Tue	Wed	Thu	Fri	Sat	Sun
		1	2	3	4	5
6	7	8	9	10	11	12
13	14	15	16	17	18	19
20	21	22	23	24	25	26
27	28	29	30	31		

August 2020

Mon	Tue	Wed	Thu	Fri	Sat	Sun
					1	2
3	4	5	6	7	8	9
10	11	12	13	14	15	16
17	18	19	20	21	22	23
24	25	26	27	28	29	30
31						

September 2020

Mon	Tue	Wed	Thu	Fri	Sat	Sun
	1	2	3	4	5	6
7	8	9	10	11	12	13
14	15	16	17	18	19	20
21	22	23	24	25	26	27
28	29	30				

October 2020

Mon	Tue	Wed	Thu	Fri	Sat	Sun
			1	2	3	4
5	6	7	8	9	10	11
12	13	14	15	16	17	18
19	20	21	22	23	24	25
26	27	28	29	30	31	

November 2020

Mon	Tue	Wed	Thu	Fri	Sat	Sun
						1
2	3	4	5	6	7	8
9	10	11	12	13	14	15
16	17	18	19	20	21	22
23	24	25	26	27	28	29
30						

December 2020

Mon	Tue	Wed	Thu	Fri	Sat	Sun
	1	2	3	4	5	6
7	8	9	10	11	12	13
14	15	16	17	18	19	20
21	22	23	24	25	26	27
28	29	30	31			

January 2021

Mon	Tue	Wed	Thu	Fri	Sat	Sun
				1	2	3
4	5	6	7	8	9	10
11	12	13	14	15	16	17
18	19	20	21	22	23	24
25	26	27	28	29	30	31

February 2021

Mon	Tue	Wed	Thu	Fri	Sat	Sun
1	2	3	4	5	6	7
8	9	10	11	12	13	14
15	16	17	18	19	20	21
22	23	24	25	26	27	28

March 2021

Mon	Tue	Wed	Thu	Fri	Sat	Sun
1	2	3	4	5	6	7
8	9	10	11	12	13	14
15	16	17	18	19	20	21
22	23	24	25	26	27	28
29	30	31				

April 2021

Mon	Tue	Wed	Thu	Fri	Sat	Sun
			1	2	3	4
5	6	7	8	9	10	11
12	13	14	15	16	17	18
19	20	21	22	23	24	25
26	27	28	29	30		

May 2021

Mon	Tue	Wed	Thu	Fri	Sat	Sun
					1	2
3	4	5	6	7	8	9
10	11	12	13	14	15	16
17	18	19	20	21	22	23
24	25	26	27	28	29	30
31						

June 2021

Mon	Tue	Wed	Thu	Fri	Sat	Sun
	1	2	3	4	5	6
7	8	9	10	11	12	13
14	15	16	17	18	19	20
21	22	23	24	25	26	27
28	29	30				

July 2021

Mon	Tue	Wed	Thu	Fri	Sat	Sun
			1	2	3	4
5	6	7	8	9	10	11
12	13	14	15	16	17	18
19	20	21	22	23	24	25
26	27	28	29	30	31	

August 2021

Mon	Tue	Wed	Thu	Fri	Sat	Sun
						1
2	3	4	5	6	7	8
9	10	11	12	13	14	15
16	17	18	19	20	21	22
23	24	25	26	27	28	29
30	31					

Your university's key dates

Registration

Inductions

Freshers' week

Field trips

Study/reading week(s)

Graduation dates

Summer school

Semester/Term dates

Semester/Term 1   Finish

Semester/Term 2   Finish

Semester/Term 3   Finish

Semester/Term 4   Finish

Examination dates

Semester/Term 1 exams begin   Finish

Semester/Term 2 exams begin   Finish

Semester/Term 3 exams begin   Finish

Semester/Term 4 exams begin   Finish

Resit exams begin   Finish

Holiday dates

Winter vacation   Finish

Spring vacation   Finish

Summer vacation   Finish

Next academic year

Registration dates

Additional key dates/notes

7

Public holidays and notable dates 2020–21

Dates have been obtained from UK sources where possible. Religious festivals have been verified from a variety of international sources taking into account variations in dates according to location and country. Please confirm the dates appropriate to you through your local religious group.

Bank and public holidays

Summer Bank Holiday (Scotland)	3 August 2020	St Patrick's Day (Ireland)	17 March 2021
Summer Bank Holiday UK (except Scotland)	31 August 2020	Good Friday	2 April 2021
St Andrew's Day Bank Holiday (Scotland)	30 November 2020	Easter Monday Bank Holiday UK (except Scotland)	5 April 2021
Christmas Day	25 December 2020	Early May Bank Holiday	3 May 2021
Boxing Day	26 December 2020	Spring Bank Holiday	31 May 2021
Boxing Day holiday	28 December 2020	Bank Holiday (Northern Ireland)	12 July 2021
New Year's Day	1 January 2021	Summer Bank Holiday (Scotland)	2 August 2021
Bank Holiday (Scotland)	4 January 2021	Summer Bank Holiday (except Scotland)	30 August 2021

Notable dates
International days

United Nations Day	24 October 2020	Commonwealth Day	8 March 2021
Human Rights Day	10 December 2020	World Environment Day	5 June 2021
Holocaust Memorial Day	27 January 2021	World Population Day	11 July 2021

UK secular cultural dates and observances

Autumnal Equinox	22 September 2020	Burns' Night (Scotland)	25 January 2021
British Summer Time (BST) ends	25 October 2020	Vernal Equinox	20 March 2021
Guy Fawkes'/Bonfire Night	5 November 2020	British Summer Time (BST) begins	28 March 2021
Winter Solstice/Yule	21 December 2020	Father's Day	20 June 2021
New Year's Eve	31 December 2020	Summer Solstice	21 June 2021

Religious festivals by world religions

Bahá'í

Birth of the Báb	17–18 October 2020
Birth of Bahá'u'lláh	19 October 2020
Day of the Covenant	25 November 2020
Ascension of 'Abdu'l-Bahá	27 November 2020
World Religion Day	17 January 2021
Naw-Rúz/New Year	20 March 2021
First Day of Ridván	20 April 2021
Ninth Day of Ridván	28 April 2021
Last Day of Ridván	2 May 2021
Declaration of the Báb	23 May 2021
Ascension of Bahá'u'lláh	28 May 2021
Martyrdom of the Báb	9 July 2021

Buddhist

Obon/Ullambana	13–15 August 2020
Bodhi Day/Rohatsu	8 December 2020
Mahayana New Year	28 January 2021
Chinese New Year	12 February 2021
Nirvana Day	15 February 2021
Magha Puja Day	27 February 2021
Theravada New Year	27 April 2021
Visakha Puja/Buddha Day	18 May 2021
Obon/Ullambana	13–15 July 2021
Asalha Puja Day	24 July 2021

Christian

Lammas	1 August 2020
Nativity of the Virgin Mary	8 September 2020
Feast of St Michael and All Angels	29 September 2020
St Francis of Assisi Day	4 October 2020
Feast of St Luke	18 October 2020
All Hallows' Eve (Hallowe'en)	31 October 2020
All Saints' Day	1 November 2020
First Sunday in Advent	29 November 2020
St Andrew's Day	30 November 2020
St Nicholas' Day	6 December 2020
Christmas Eve	24 December 2020
Christmas Day	25 December 2020
Twelfth Night	5 January 2021
Epiphany	6 January 2021
Baptism of Christ	10 January 2021
Candlemas/Presentation of Christ in the Temple	2 February 2021
St Valentine's Day	14 February 2021
Shrove Tuesday	16 February 2021
Ash Wednesday	17 February 2021
St David's Day	1 March 2021
Mothering Sunday	14 March 2021
St Patrick's Day	17 March 2021
Palm Sunday	28 March 2021
Good Friday	2 April 2021
Easter Day	4 April 2021
St George's Day	23 April 2021
Ascension Day	13 May 2021
Trinity Sunday	30 May 2021
Corpus Christi	3 June 2021
Pentecost	20 June 2021
Feast Day of St Peter and St Paul	29 June 2021
Lammas	1 August 2021

Confucian/Daoist

Chinese New Year	12 February 2021

Hindu

Raksha Bandhan	3 August 2020
Krishna Janmashtami	11 August 2020
Raksha Bandhan	21 August 2021
Ganesh Chaturthi	22 August 2020
Krishna Janmashtami	29 August 2021
Navaratri	17–24 October 2020
Dasara	25 October 2020
Diwali	14 November 2020
Vikram New Year	15 November 2020

Interfaith

Thanksgiving (Canada)	12 October 2020
Remembrance Sunday	8 November 2020
Thanksgiving (USA)	26 November 2020
Father's Day	20 June 2021

Islam

Waqf al Arafa	29 July 2020
Eid al Adha	31 July–3 August 2020
Al-Hijra/New Year	20 August 2020
Ashura	29 August 2020
Mawlid an Nabi	29 October 2020
Laylat al Miraj	10 March 2021
Laylat al Bara'at	28 March 2021
Ramadan	12 April – 12 May 2021
Laylat al Qadr	8 May 2021
Eid al Fitr	12–13 May 2021
Waqf al Arafa	19 July 2021
Eid al Adha	20–23 July 2021
Al-Hijra/New Year	10 August 2021
Ashura	18 August 2021

Jain

Paryushana Parva	16 August 2020
New Year	14 November 2020
Diwali	14 November 2020
Nirvana Day	15 February 2021
Mahavir Jayanti	25 April 2021

Jewish

Tish'a B'Av	29–30 July 2020
Rosh Hashanah/New Year	19–20 September 2020
Yom Kippur/Day of Atonement	28 September 2020
Sukkot/Feast of Tabernacles	3–9 October 2020
Shemini Atzeret	10 October 2020
Simchat Torah	11 October 2020
Hanukkah	11–18 December 2020
Tu BiShvat	28 January 2021
Purim	26 February 2021
Pesach/Passover	27 March – 4 April 2021
Yom HaShoah/Holocaust Memorial Day	8 April 2021
Yom HaAtzma'ut	15 April 2021
Lag B'Omer	30 April 2021
Shavuot/Feast of Weeks	10–18 May 2021
Tish'a B'Av	18 July 2021

Pagan

Lammas	1 August 2020
Winter Solstice/Yule	21 December 2020
Beltane	1 May 2021
Lammas	1 August 2021

Scientology

Birthday of L. Ron Hubbard	13 March 2021

Sikh

Installation of Scriptures as Guru Granth Sahib	20 October 2020
Diwali	14 November 2020
Martyrdom of Guru Tegh Bahadur	24 November 2020
Birthday of Guru Nanak Dev	30 November 2020
Birthday of Guru Gobind Singh	5 January 2021
Maghi	13 January 2021
Hola Mohalla	29 March 2021
Baisakhi/Vaisakhi	13 April 2021
Martyrdom of Guru Arjan Dev	16 June 2021

Wicca

Winter Solstice/Yule	21 December 2020
Litha	22 June 2021

Additional dates/festivals important to you

University may initially seem strange compared with schools or colleges. Some features may be similar, while others could be completely new to you. If you are a fresher or transferring from another institution, this brief description of the main structures and key players may help you understand this learning environment.

- **The Chancellor** is the titular head of the institution, but will have a largely ceremonial role, for example conferring degrees at graduation.
- **The Vice-Chancellor** (Principal in Scotland) is the day-to-day Chief Executive of the institution, with a role in dictating policy, chairing committees and appointing key staff.

Generally, students don't have dealings with either of these people. On a day-to-day basis, you will interact with:

- **Senior lecturers, lecturers, assistant lecturers and research assistants,** who have responsibilities in research, teaching and administration.
- **Tutors and/or demonstrators,** who provide teaching and support in small-group learning.
- **Professors,** who are academics who have shown particular merit in teaching and/or research.
- **A head of school or department,** who is in charge of a subject unit – its staff, policies, curriculum and research. A school is generally a larger version of a department, possibly covering a broader subject area. Sometimes schools or departments are collected into faculties. Departments are supported by administrators, secretaries, technicians and IT staff.

Your role as a student

- You will follow a course of study for a degree for which attendance and exam passes in specific subjects will be required.
- Your study year will be divided into semesters or terms possibly corresponding to the length of courses or modules. You may or may not have a choice over which modules to study; often modules are prescribed for specific degrees whereas, in other cases, there may be flexibility.
- You may be represented at school/department by a staff–student liaison committee (or similar) and it is expected that staff collect student feedback and respond to it in various committee structures, most of which have some form of student representation. In some universities the students may be represented at the highest levels by an independent elected person, such as a rector.

The course handbook

- Explains how your course is organised, including the use of the class virtual learning environment (VLE) if applicable.
- Provides information about the staff teaching your modules.
- Outlines the syllabus (topics and their order) and modes of assessment for each module and exam dates.
- Includes learning objectives (outcomes) for each part of your course. These describe what staff expect you to be able to accomplish in assessments, including exams. These objectives should help you to align your revision with the material that is taught.

Assessment

- **Continuous assessment** is usually based on coursework assignments as well as outcomes of tutorials and labs.
- **Exams** may take place at the end of modules and/or at the end of the academic year. Clearly, planning ahead for these is important so you can revise the material covered and/or submit assignments on time. There is a key role for this *Planner* in that task.
- **Monitoring** of assignment and exam marking is carried out by external examiners who have a key role in the quality assurance of university degrees. From time to time, the quality of teaching and associated administration may be audited.

The rhythm of the university year

Each university year has a distinct cycle. In rough order, the key events in the academic year are as follows:

1. **Induction and freshers' weeks.** These events are designed to help orientate new students (freshers).
2. **Teaching weeks.** These cover courses or modules in a term or semester structure. These may include study weeks and probably assignment deadlines. The timetable for each subject will be given in the course handbook. It is unlikely that you will be prompted to attend each session – you'll have to organise yourself to arrive at the right location and at the right time.
3. **Exam weeks.** Again, it's your responsibility to attend at the right place or time, having studied the appropriate material.
4. **Reading weeks.** These involve a break in teaching, in theory, allowing you to catch up with your studies or complete essay and project work.
5. **Vacation.** The first vacation will be over Christmas and New Year. Whether you have exams before or after this will depend on your institution.
6. **More teaching weeks.** These contain new courses/modules, and also potentially study/reading weeks and exams.
7. **Vacation.** The second vacation is usually over the Easter period. Again, modules may be split over this break.
8. **Year and degree exams.** Details differ between universities. You may be given a generous allowance of time for revision, but you may also face a number of exams in close sequence. Planning is vital! Some exams may be done online.
9. **Summer vacation.** In most institutions, this is a lengthier break, during which the academics will often be researching or attending conferences. You may wish to find employment during this period to top up your finances. Increasingly, universities are offering modules during these times with the aim of speeding up degree courses.
10. **Resits.** These are opportunities for students to sit exams again in case of failure.

Course overview

The generalised annual cycle outlined above repeats for two, three or four years depending on your degree, entry level of place of study. Specifics of your course will involve the following:

- Your study topics will become more detailed and complex at each successive level.
- Teaching sessions will consist of a mix of lectures, practicals and tutorials as deemed appropriate for your subject.
- Various in-course assignments will be given to allow you to gain feedback on the standard of your work.
- You may also be expected to complete a dissertation or research project, especially in your final year.
- The regulations for each degree will require that you pass specific modules. At 'honours' level (your final year) a grade may be given based on your course marks. In descending order this could be first class, upper second, lower second, third class and pass.
- Graduations occur usually before the summer vacation and often between terms/semesters in the winter. These ceremonies are joyous family occasions that make all the effort in studying for your degree seem worthwhile. Following a degree, you may wish to study for a 'masters', a doctorate or other advanced qualification (and some degrees, like medicine, have such opportunities embedded in the 'normal' curriculum).

Should the above seem complex, this *Planner* is designed to simplify things for you, to help you record the key upcoming events and to help you get organised for assignments and exams.

We wish you all the best in your studies!

University postal address

You'll find location details of university facilities on your campus map.

Academic registry

Academic support services

Admissions office

Campus bank/ATM

Campus bookshop

Chaplaincy

Childcare services

Counselling services

Disability advisory service

Employment & careers office

Faculty/school office

Finance/cash office

Financial advice office

Gym/sports facilities   1   2

International office

IT suite

Lecture building(s)

Main library

Reception/information desk

Residences/accommodation office

Student help desk/nightline

Students' Union

Subject libraries   1   2

Tutorial/lab work building

University health centre

Additional locations:

Accommodation details

Landlord/university accommodation office

Name	
Address	
	Postcode
Phone	Mobile
Email	
Start of tenancy	End of tenancy
Date deposit paid	Amount paid
Rent payment dates	
Inventory signed	
Contact code:	Mobile:

Important services

Note contact details for services you may need, e.g. utilities

Emergency contacts

	1. In case of emergency, please contact	2. In case of emergency, please contact
Name		
Relationship		
Home phone		
Work phone		
Mobile		
Email		
Postal address		
Postcode		

Be sure you add your personal details on the page of publication details at the beginning of the *Student Planner & University Diary*.

First week checklist – all students

Catch up with administration at university and department/school

- ❑ Attend any induction meetings
- ❑ Review course or module-specific information provided by your department/school
- ❑ Meet your Adviser of Studies (sometimes called Personal Tutor or Director of Studies) to discuss course and module options
- ❑ Matriculate (register/enrol) as instructed. Returning students may use an online process
- ❑ Pay any fees as necessary
- ❑ Obtain your student identity card (sometimes called 'Matriculation Card')

Organise yourself for the semester/term

- ❑ Find out your timetable for classes and enter in the term planner (see pages 268–270)
- ❑ Find out about important assessment deadlines, exam deadlines and other appointments and enter these in the diary section (see also university's key dates)
- ❑ Check address details, phone numbers and email addresses for
  - Adviser of Studies (Personal Tutor/Director of Studies)
  - Departmental (school) offices
  - University library
  - General practitioner/dentist/university health service (make sure you have your NHS card – UK students only)
  - Landlord or accommodation services

  Enter contact details in the relevant section of this planner
- ❑ Join or rejoin societies, clubs and sports facilities/gym

Organise yourself for the first week

- ❑ Review all of the university documentation sent to you for important dates and times
- ❑ Use the diary section of this book to make a note from these documents of all the appointments, events and activities relevant to you
- ❑ Plan what you are going to do each day as far as you can

Additional notes

Attend to your accommodation needs as appropriate

☐ Book into accommodation

☐ Before signing the inventory, check equipment is all there and in good order and note any damage or omissions. This will be important when reclaiming your deposit

☐ Identify extra things that you may need to purchase for comfort and convenience

☐ If applicable, contact utilities (gas, electricity, phone, water) regarding connection or reconnection

☐ Make sure you know the fire drill where relevant

☐ Arrange insurance cover. If your accommodation fee does not include insurance cover, arrange specific contents insurance for yourself. The Students' Union can provide information about companies that offer specific cover for students

Plan your travel arrangements

☐ Apply for or renew student travel cards for bus, rail, tram, underground as appropriate

☐ Apply for campus parking permit if available to students and if appropriate

☐ Apply for local parking season ticket if needed

☐ Check journey times to and from the university at relevant times of day and night

Contact local government and services

☐ Arrange through the local council office for your details to be added to or amended on the Electoral Register

☐ Register with a local GP practice (or re-register, if you've moved)

☐ Register with a local dental practice (or re-register, if you've moved)

Organising yourself – preparation checklist

Things you'll need	Things you need to do

First week checklist – for freshers and students transferring from other institutions

- ❑ Read your university freshers' pack introduction, including information sent from the Students' Union
- ❑ Attend freshers' week events – both academic and social
- ❑ Attend welcome from Vice-Chancellor/Principal
- ❑ Go on a campus tour and a city or town tour
- ❑ Get to grips with the geography/organisation of your university – study the campus map
- ❑ Find on-campus facilities, e.g. library, sports hall, chaplaincy, parking zones
- ❑ Join the library and sign up for and attend induction tour
- ❑ Attend IT induction/registration and log into IT account, changing password as necessary
- ❑ Sign up for additional IT training as appropriate
- ❑ Check that your virtual learning environment (VLE) includes information for the correct modules/courses
- ❑ Attend induction lectures for your course(s) as appropriate
- ❑ Attend Societies' Fayre
- ❑ Research special student deals (e.g. banking) and loyalty card offers
- ❑ Get personal safety leaflets and details of other services as applicable
- ❑ Be safe. Buy a personal alarm (often available cheaply at Students' Union shop)

Additional notes

Your university life

Your relationship with your university involves expectations and responsibilities on both sides. These interactions with staff and other students will define and shape your learning experience and ultimately your career path. These tips focus on organisational and administrative aspects of the student experience, helping you to orientate yourself within your academic community.

Your personal life

Many students have home duties, family responsibilities and work obligations that impact on their academic lives. Achieving a realistic balance between academic and personal roles is an important aspect of the university experience. These tips are designed to help you to achieve this balanced approach.

Academic literacy

An understanding of what is required of you in higher education is essential so you can achieve your full potential. This awareness and development of academic competence is called 'academic literacy'. This strand of tips also covers various high-level thinking skills required at university.

Studying and learning

The activities of studying and learning are, of course, a vital part of higher education. However, it's important not to rely solely on methods assimilated at school or college. As you progress through the university system, you will need to develop a wider range of higher-level skills. These tips will help you advance your technique in this area to meet university standards.

Working on course assessments

According to research, there are over 64 different types of academic writing assessments that students might be required to complete. In addition, other non-written performance may be assessed. These include oral presentations, tutorial discussions and subject-specific practical activities including problem-solving. This set of tips helps with aspects of these assessed activities.

Dealing with exams

University examinations are conducted in a range of formats, for example, online exams with multiple choice questions (MCQs), short answer questions (SAQs), conventional written (essay-style) papers or oral interviews. These tips will help you to plan for revision and exam sitting, whatever the mode of assessment.

Reflecting and planning

Effective learners reflect on their experiences as part of the process of their development and the achievement of graduate status. This involves planning for further learning and employability, a process that assists in the fulfilment of future academic and career goals. These tips deal with this vital aspect of being a successful student and graduate.

ACADEMIC DIARY
2020-21

Monday	Tuesday	Wednesday
27	28	29
3	4	5
10	11	12
17	18	19
24	25	26

Thursday	Friday	Saturday/Sunday
30	31	1
		2
6	7	8
		9
13	14	15
		16
20	21	22
		23
27	28	29
		30

Things to do this month

At this time in the academic year you will probably be . . .

. . . gathering all the paperwork you will need to take to university.

Organise a folder containing all the documents you will need once you arrive. This might include: letter of acceptance, birth certificate, passport, driving licence, bank details, loan confirmation letters, insurance documents, medical card, list of contact information. See **Planning Resource 1.1** for a checklist of further items you may require.

. . . ensuring your loan, bursary or grant entitlements are in place.

Look over information you have been sent and check your entitlement. If appropriate, find out details of bursary and scholarship programmes to see whether you qualify. Make sure that you have sent off all the necessary forms before the cut-off date(s).

. . . planning what you will need to organise your study materials.

Choose a method for filing your notes – both those you make yourself and those that may be taken or given out in lectures. A couple of large lever arch files (with card dividers) are probably a good investment as you can then sub-divide paperwork by theme, topic or lecturer. Buy good quality files; they'll last longer. In addition, you'll need to devise a system for storing learning materials electronically.

. . . considering how much time you are expected to study.

Independent working is a key element of university study. A full-time student is expected to spend a full working week studying in formal lectures, labs, tutorials and other practical work as well as on private study, preparation and e-learning activities. Module timetables may show only a few hours of lectures, labs and tutorials per week, but you will also need to allow time for reading around the subject, preparation for tutorials, labs, writing for in-course assessments and other compulsory activities.

. . . reviewing the course information that you have been given.

Examine the course handbook, reading list and other print/online resources. Try to obtain a flavour of the course, the types of learning activities involved and consider how comfortable you are with these. Good planning and time management are essential to ensure you perform well – **Planning Resources 2.1, 2.2 and 3.1** templates may help.

. . . thinking about how your learning will be assessed.

Be prepared to experience different types of assessment at university; depending on your subject, these may be time-restricted online multiple choice type, formal written exams, essay-type assignments, reports or short answer questions. Note that exams are unique to each institution, but, at this stage, be aware that past papers may only become meaningful once you have started the course.

. . . thinking about your long-term goals.

You may be about to make subject choices that could impact on your career after graduation. Think carefully about how the course will support any career aims you might have and ensure that your choices do not restrict your career options. Your personal development plan may help (see **Planning Resource 6.3**). Your Adviser of Studies (Personal Tutor/Director of Studies) will be able to advise on career-compatible choices.

27 Monday

🕐	What	Where
To do		

28 Tuesday

🕐	What	Where
To do		

Tish'a B'Av (Jewish)
Waqf al Arafa (Islam)

29 Wednesday

🕐	What	Where
To do		

30 Thursday

Tish'a B'Av (Jewish)

🕐	What	Where
To do		

31 Friday

Eid al Adha begins (Islam)

🕐	What	Where
To do		

1 Saturday   Lammas (Christian/Pagan)

2 Sunday

Tip of the week

Sort out your semester-time accommodation as quickly as possible. Try to do this before you arrive on campus, if you can. The best (and/or cheaper) places will be in demand, and you may miss out because others have registered their interest first. **Planning Resource 1.2** is a checklist of aspects to take into account.

Summer Bank Holiday (Scotland)
Eid al Adha ends (Islam)   Raksha Bandhan (Hindu)

3 Monday

🕐	What	Where
To do	

4 Tuesday

🕐	What	Where
To do	

5 Wednesday

🕐	What	Where
To do	

6 Thursday

🕐	What	Where
To do		

7 Friday

🕐	What	Where
To do		

8 Saturday

9 Sunday

💡 Tip of the week

If you're leaving home to be at university, you'll need a good packing list to include everything you'll need and so avoid having to buy duplicate items. A checklist is provided in **Planning Resource 1.1**.

10 Monday

🕐	What	Where
To do		

11 Tuesday

Krishna Janmashtami (Hindu)

🕐	What	Where
To do		

12 Wednesday

🕐	What	Where
To do		

13 Thursday
Obon/Ullambana begins (Buddhist)

🕐	What	Where
To do		

14 Friday

🕐	What	Where
To do		

15 Saturday
Obon/Ullambana ends (Buddhist)

16 Sunday
Paryushana Parva (Jain)

💡 Tip of the week

Set up a draft financial budget for the academic year. This will only be as good as the information that goes into it, so it is important to estimate income and expenses as accurately as possible. **Planning Resources 1.3 and 1.4** may be helpful.

17 Monday

🕐	What	Where
To do		

18 Tuesday

🕐	What	Where
To do		

19 Wednesday

🕐	What	Where
To do		

20 Thursday
Al-Hijra/New Year (Islam)

🕐	What	Where
To do		

21 Friday

🕐	What	Where
To do		

22 Saturday Ganesh Chaturthi (Hindu)

23 Sunday

Tip of the week

Once you begin university, don't forget to maintain contacts outside the university – you may be so drawn into university activities that you let these slip. Keeping in contact by emailing, texting, social networking or phoning is important for everyone.

24 Monday

🕐	What	Where
To do		

25 Tuesday

🕐	What	Where
To do		

26 Wednesday

🕐	What	Where
To do		

27 Thursday

🕐	What	Where
To do		

28 Friday

🕐	What	Where
To do		

29 Saturday   Ashura (Islam)   ## 30 Sunday

Tip of the week

If you find you are struggling with *any* aspect of your coursework, relationships, mental or physical health, *do not hesitate* to seek help from advisers or specialist services at your university. They are paid to help and your visit will be confidential. Moreover, any interventions necessary will not affect your course grades or academic record.

Monday	Tuesday	Wednesday
31	1	2
7	8	9
14	15	16
21	22	23
28	29	30

Thursday	Friday	Saturday/Sunday
3	4	5
		6
10	11	12
		13
17	18	19
		20
24	25	26
		27
1	2	3
		4

Things to do this month

At this time in the academic year you will probably be . . .

. . . entering or re-entering the learning community of university.

Although, initially, you may cover some old ground in lectures, look out for enhanced detail and different modes of presentation, terminology and emphasis. Lecturers will probably take you further than your previous studies using your 'old' knowledge as a foundation for new and potentially different types of learning and ways of receiving information. Remain open-minded about alternative approaches; be prepared to learn from them.

. . . prioritising tasks.

Use the daily 'To do' spaces in this planner to list all the things that need to be done in your academic and personal life so you prioritise and order them through the day. You might adopt a numerical ranking system or one using stars to arrange the order of importance. Scoring off completed items gives a sense of achievement and of being in control of the calls on your time (see also **Planning Resource 2.2**).

. . . reviewing your learning skills for university.

Make enquiries about inductions or short courses to develop your independent learning skills at university. These facilities exist because people sometimes need a little help, so do ask as soon as possible rather than just muddling through. Look for information on the university home page on:
– IT Support Services for help with word-processing, software packages, keyboard skills and e-learning portals.
– Library for familiarisation/induction programmes and guidance on information literacy.
– Learning Support Centre for advice on learning including refresher maths, academic writing or exam techniques (**Planning Resources 3.5–3.7, 5.3, 5.5 and 7.1–7.7**).

. . . learning how to make the lecture room 'work' for you.

Arrive as early as possible so you can choose where you sit, rather than having to take a seat where there is noise from air-conditioning vents or back-row chatterers. A clear view of the lecturer and display facilities is essential.

. . . creating deadlines while building flexibility into your planning.

Take into account that you may have more than one assignment due around the same time. Set yourself a finishing date for each that is ahead of the formal submission deadline (**Planning Resources 2.1 and 3.1**). That way you will have the luxury of time to review your work, correct errors and improve the quality of presentation.

. . . planning ahead for exams.

At an early stage you should think about how you will be assessed. A key activity is to look at the intended learning outcomes for your course as the component teaching elements take place. Reviewing marking criteria and past exam papers can also help you to get a feel for the standards required.

. . . trying to establish ways of making best use of your time.

University courses assume a full working week. Over a week, write down how you spend your time. This will show how long you take for particular activities and also how productive time can evaporate. Identify when you are at your 'learning best' (day/evening) and try to plan intensive study activities to optimise this, while keeping more mundane tasks for less productive times (see **Planning Resource 2.2** for further tips).

31 Monday

🕐	What	Where
To do		

1 Tuesday

🕐	What	Where
To do		

2 Wednesday

🕐	What	Where
To do		

3 Thursday

🕐	What	Where
To do		

4 Friday

🕐	What	Where
To do		

5 Saturday

6 Sunday

💡 Tip of the week

Before you begin your studies, think about how you may need to change your approach to learning when studying in new ways, in new locations, with new people and with new or modified methods for advanced study at university. Consider what adjustments you may need to make. If you're a returning student, think about what modifications you may need to make for more advanced study.

7 Monday

🕐	What	Where
To do		

Nativity of the
Virgin Mary (Christian)

8 Tuesday

🕐	What	Where
To do		

9 Wednesday

🕐	What	Where
To do		

10 Thursday

🕐	What	Where
To do		

11 Friday

🕐	What	Where
To do		

12 Saturday

13 Sunday

💡 Tip of the week

Think about the balance you're aiming for between study and social activities. How do you plan to achieve a suitable allocation of your time and energy? How will you know if you're attaining this? This Planner might be a useful place to create plans for, and records of, your activities. You should review these frequently.

14 Monday

🕐	What	Where
To do		

15 Tuesday

🕐	What	Where
To do		

16 Wednesday

🕐	What	Where
To do		

17 Thursday

🕐	What	Where
To do		

18 Friday

🕐	What	Where
To do		

19 Saturday Rosh Hashanah/ New Year begins (Jewish)

20 Sunday Rosh Hashanah/ New Year ends (Jewish)

Tip of the week

At the start of a new academic year, be ready to set your own rules, routines and methods of working to achieve your goals. No-one else will be dictating what you should do, or when, so it's up to you to take the initiative (see **Planning Resource 1.5**).

21 Monday

🕐	What	Where
To do		

22 Tuesday

Autumnal Equinox

🕐	What	Where
To do		

23 Wednesday

🕐	What	Where
To do		

24 Thursday

🕐	What	Where
To do		

25 Friday

🕐	What	Where
To do		

26 Saturday

27 Sunday

💡 Tip of the week

Make sure you are fully prepared when visiting your Academic Adviser (may also be called Adviser/Director of Studies or Personal Tutor) – be ready to discuss your proposed course, degree and career options when you register (matriculate/enrol).

Monthly planner

Monday	Tuesday	Wednesday
28	29	30
5	6	7
12	13	14
19	20	21
26	27	28

Thursday	Friday	Saturday/Sunday
1	2	3
		4
8	9	10
		11
15	16	17
		18
22	23	24
		25
29	30	31
		1

Things to do this month

At this time in the academic year you will probably be . . .

. . . thinking about the expectations of teaching staff.

Academic staff will be prompting you to prepare for lectures, tutorials or practicals by reading handouts beforehand. You will also be expected to work independently by reading around your subject. Find out whether you will be expected to download online slides and handouts in preparation for classes. These materials are often available through your institution's virtual learning environment (VLE).

. . . reviewing the reality of your expenditure.

Revisit your draft budget (**Planning Resource 1.4**) and put in more accurate figures that reflect the true costs of life as a student. For example, factor printing costs into your budget. Keep costs down by taking advantage of special student reductions, but look carefully at the small print before you sign up for some offers as they may tie you into a longer-term expense.

. . . managing your source material effectively to avoid plagiarism.

Always note down all the reference information required to locate hard copy or electronic source material – you will probably need it at a later point. Typically, you should note the author(s), the title, the date of publication, the publisher and the place of publication, as well as website/URL, if appropriate, so you can follow the approved referencing style (see your course handbook and **Planning Resources 4.1–4.6**).

. . . learning from your early assignments.

The first tasks may be formative (for practice), whereas later tasks will be summative (contributing to your final course mark). In either case, read the marker's annotations and written feedback carefully to see what is expected in terms of content and level (see **Planning Resources 3.5 and 3.8**). If you feel that your marks do not reflect your efforts, then arrange to see a tutor or a study adviser who can help by analysing marked work and suggesting different approaches you might take when tackling assignments and producing academic writing.

. . . safeguarding your digital files.

Make sure you keep back-ups of all work done electronically. This includes saving final versions of any submitted work so that you can produce additional copies if required to do so, for example, for the external examiner to review. If using a memory stick, mark with your contact details so that it can be returned to you if it is mislaid.

. . . working with others to verify your understanding of the course.

Work with fellow students on your course to compare notes, and to confirm understanding of more difficult points. As a group, discuss potential exam questions, then draft and review potential answers. This can help the learning of all involved, as these activities contribute to the consolidation of learning and help identify gaps in knowledge and technique (see e.g. **Planning Resource 5.5**).

. . . thinking afresh about your goals and aspirations.

To help with this, try answering the following questions, in sequence:
1. Where would you like to be, career-wise, in ten years' time?
2. What sort of degree will you need to get on the first step of that career ladder?
3. What steps can you take within this semester to help towards your degree goals?

28 Monday
Yom Kippur/Day of Atonement (Jewish)

⏰	What	Where
To do		

29 Tuesday
Feast of St Michael and All Angels (Christian)

⏰	What	Where
To do		

30 Wednesday

⏰	What	Where
To do		

1 Thursday

🕐	What	Where
To do		

2 Friday

🕐	What	Where
To do		

3 Saturday — Sukkot/Feast of Tabernacles begins (Jewish)

4 Sunday — St Francis of Assisi Day (Christian)

Tip of the week

Try to get to know your fellow students. For example, you might aim to introduce yourself to a 'new' person every day. If living in halls, avoid going home at weekends so you can attend social events and meet new people; if living at home, try to become involved in university life, e.g. by joining clubs and studying on campus.

5 Monday

🕐	What	Where
To do		

6 Tuesday

🕐	What	Where
To do		

7 Wednesday

🕐	What	Where
To do		

8 Thursday

🕐	What	Where
To do		

9 Friday   Sukkot/Feast of Tabernacles ends (Jewish)

🕐	What	Where
To do		

10 Saturday   Shemini Atzeret (Jewish)   11 Sunday   Simchat Torah (Jewish)

Tip of the week

Plan ahead to get the most out of your course. Using this planner, and referring to your course handbook, map out the routine things you'll need to do each day, every week and also to meet special deadlines (see **Planning Resources 2.1, 2.2 and 3.1**).

12 Monday

Thanksgiving (Canada) (Interfaith)

🕐	What	Where
To do		

13 Tuesday

🕐	What	Where
To do		

14 Wednesday

🕐	What	Where
To do		

15 Thursday

🕐	What	Where
To do		

16 Friday

🕐	What	Where
To do		

17 Saturday   Birth of the Báb (Bahá'í) Navaratri begins (Hindu)

18 Sunday   Feast of St Luke (Christian)

💡 **Tip of the week**

Take time at the start of each module to explore the online resources available to you. Get into a daily routine of visiting your VLE (virtual learning environment) and carrying out related study tasks such as responding to email or taking part in discussion boards (see **Planning Resource 2.7**).

October 2020

19 Monday
Birth of Bahá'u'lláh (Bahá'í)

🕐	What	Where
To do		

20 Tuesday
Installation of Scriptures as Guru Granth Sahib (Sikh)

🕐	What	Where
To do		

21 Wednesday

🕐	What	Where
To do		

22 Thursday

🕐	What	Where
To do		

23 Friday

🕐	What	Where
To do		

24 Saturday   United Nations Day
Navaratri ends (Hindu)

25 Sunday   Dasara (Hindu)
British Summer Time
(BST) ends

💡 Tip of the week

Organise your computer files. Create separate folders for each topic within the course you are studying, and save your material using a file-name that will make sense to you even when you need to locate it several months later. Remember to make frequent back-ups!

Monday	Tuesday	Wednesday
26	27	28
2	3	4
9	10	11
16	17	18
23	24	25

Thursday	Friday	Saturday/Sunday
29	30	31
		1
5	6	7
		8
12	13	14
		15
19	20	21
		22
26	27	28
		29

Things to do this month

At this time in the academic year you will probably be . . .

. . . participating in online discussions.

Make the most of opportunities through online discussion boards to take part in informal, focused debate on issues arising in your courses. You can learn a lot simply by putting your thoughts into words. This helps develop critical thinking and your contribution shows your engagement with the subject matter.

. . . reflecting on the impact of university on other aspects of your life.

Focus on your learning needs by organising your study periods so that you can create new social networks and maintain established ones. Explain to people around you what these learning commitments require of you. Talking about these demands can help others to maintain a balanced perspective on your studies.

. . . developing your professional vocabulary.

Systematically note down new discipline-specific words and their meanings. Record them in alphabetical order in a glossary (e.g. **Planning Resource 2.5**), as this makes retrieval and spell-checking easier. Also develop your own 'shorthand' for specialist terms for use in note-taking in lectures and note-making from your reading.

. . . ensuring that your learning is 'active learning'.

If you find that you are studying large chunks of material and that none of it is 'sticking', evolve alternative ways in which you might learn the material. For example, alter the length of your study periods or vary the type of material you work on over a learning period so that your mind does not lapse into 'autopilot'.

. . . tackling academic assignments.

Break larger tasks down into steps so each smaller part becomes an end in itself and its completion marks a step closer to finishing the work (see **Planning Resource 3.1**). Analyse the instruction word(s) carefully (see **Planning Resource 2.6**), brainstorm your first ideas either as a list or as a mind-map, do some of the reading, then continue to expand your notes until you feel you can create a plan. Write to the plan in order to achieve a first draft, then edit, proof-read and submit (see **Planning Resource 3.7**).

. . . thinking about the prospect of end-of-module exams.

Ensure that you know when and where these will take place, especially if this is before the winter vacation. Identify the format of each exam and create a revision timetable to follow (see **Planning Resources 5.1–5.3**). Formulate an exam strategy and list things you'll need to take with you on the day. This will help you feel that you are in control.

. . . planning a realistic approach to your revision.

Work out the subjects to be covered, the time you can spend on revision and then plot a simple revision timetable allocating time to topics (see **Planning Resources 5.1 and 5.2**). At the next stage, check the learning outcomes, lecture allocation, topics covered in tutorials, practicals and past papers to obtain a sense of how to focus your studies. Modify your revision timetable on this basis, allowing flexibility for reviewing topics covered earlier.

26 Monday

🕐	What	Where
To do		

27 Tuesday

🕐	What	Where
To do		

28 Wednesday

🕐	What	Where
To do		

29 Thursday

Mawlid an Nabi (Islam)

🕐	What	Where
To do		

30 Friday

🕐	What	Where
To do		

31 Saturday

All Hallows' Eve/
Hallowe'en (Christian)

1 Sunday

All Saints' Day (Christian)

Tip of the week

In your studies, learn to identify the difference between a fact and someone's opinion about a fact. Reflecting on information, ideas and concepts requires the critical thinking skills that are essential at university (see **Planning Resources 2.4 and 3.3**).

2 Monday

🕐	What	Where
To do		

3 Tuesday

🕐	What	Where
To do		

4 Wednesday

🕐	What	Where
To do		

5 Thursday

Guy Fawkes'/Bonfire Night

🕐	What	Where
To do		

6 Friday

🕐	What	Where
To do		

7 Saturday

8 Sunday

Remembrance Sunday
(Interfaith)

💡 Tip of the week

When studying, work in short bursts while your concentration is at a maximum. Then, give yourself a quick break, perhaps by going for a short walk, and resume with a fresh mind. Be aware that people's attention span is only about twenty minutes so regular breaks restore your mental as well as your physical energy.

9 Monday

🕐	What	Where
To do		

10 Tuesday

🕐	What	Where
To do		

11 Wednesday

🕐	What	Where
To do		

12 Thursday

🕐	What	Where
To do		

13 Friday

🕐	What	Where
To do		

14 Saturday   Diwali (Hindu/Jain/Sikh) New Year (Jain)

15 Sunday   Vikram New Year (Hindu)

Tip of the week

If you are easily distracted from your studies, develop strategies to keep on track. Switch off sources of interruption such as mobile phone, social networking site, TV, email, music; lock your door, or 'disappear' to a quiet location (see **Planning Resource 3.2**).

16 Monday

🕐	What	Where
To do		

17 Tuesday

🕐	What	Where
To do		

18 Wednesday

🕐	What	Where
To do		

19 Thursday

🕐	What	Where
To do		

20 Friday

🕐	What	Where
To do		

21 Saturday

22 Sunday

Tip of the week

If you are seeking vacation work over the festive break, this might be a good time to think about applications. Remember to adapt your 'generic' CV to suit the specific types of job you are seeking (see **Planning Resource 6.4**).

23 Monday

🕐	What	Where
To do		

24 Tuesday

Martyrdom of Guru Tegh Bahadur (Sikh)

🕐	What	Where
To do		

25 Wednesday

Day of the Covenant (Bahá'í)

🕐	What	Where
To do		

26 Thursday
Thanksgiving (USA) (Interfaith)

🕐	What	Where
To do		

27 Friday
Ascension of ´Abdu´l-Bahá (Bahá´í)

🕐	What	Where
To do		

28 Saturday

29 Sunday
First Sunday in Advent (Christian)

Tip of the week
If you are struggling with a particular topic, go back to basics to achieve a mental framework to which your other learning can be attached. In other words, don't get obsessed with detail at this stage, just make sure you understand the bigger picture. As your studies progress, so will your understanding of challenging areas.

Monthly planner

Monday	Tuesday	Wednesday
30	1	2
7	8	9
14	15	16
21	22	23
28	29	30

Thursday	Friday	Saturday/Sunday
3	4	5
		6
10	11	12
		13
17	18	19
		20
24	25	26
		27
31	1	2
		3

At this time in the academic year you will probably be . . .

. . . pondering on work to be covered over the winter vacation.

Before you leave campus, ensure that you have access to resources you'll need to study for exams and assignments due in the next term or semester. Make a conscious decision to allocate space and time amid festive activities and seasonal employment to complete the necessary work ahead of the examination or submission dates.

. . . planning for the winter vacation period.

Make sure you relax, catch up with friends and generally 'recharge your batteries'. You may be considering taking up paid employment over the holiday period, but remember to allow time for yourself and your family.

. . . developing analytical thinking for university.

Especially in relation to exams, think beyond simple description, listing of facts, process or events. Instead, try to explain their importance and deeper implications as part of a structured appraisal of a problem and its solutions (see **Planning Resources 3.3 and 3.4**). In lectures and other learning situations, listen to the way your lecturer uses analytical thinking in presenting arguments, explaining inferences or critiquing the work of others.

. . . familiarising yourself with the work of key experts in your subject.

As you read the work of subject experts, be prepared to evaluate critically the pros and cons of their arguments and the strength of the evidence they present in support (see also **Planning Resource 3.3**). Learning that you can challenge the views, concepts or approaches of others, even those acclaimed as experts, is an important step in your university and professional training.

. . . balancing all the demands of your course.

Make sure that, even when under pressure to complete assessed work and prepare for exams, you maintain your participation in all aspects of the course. It is often the final lectures, tutorials and practicals that will help you make conceptual connections that reveal the full complexity of the themes staff have been teaching. Missing these strategically important lectures may have a significant negative impact on your understanding and exam marks.

. . . adjusting your academic writing for university-standard exams.

Get straight to the point of the question and explain your response to it as a guide to the direction your answer will take. Develop each point and draw to a tight conclusion. You cannot be expected to produce the quality of writing expected for in-course assignments, so practise writing answers against the clock to gain experience in writing succinctly and quickly for exams. This will help you in December or January exams.

. . . reflecting on your performance.

Make time during the winter vacation to reflect on the challenges you have met and how you have fared. Think about how you can build on the foundations that have been laid in the first phase of the academic year. Review the options already selected for the next study period and consider whether it might be helpful to arrange a meeting with a tutor or adviser to discuss any adjustments you feel are necessary in the light of your experience.

St Andrew's Day Bank Holiday (Scotland)
Birthday of Guru Nanak Dev (Sikh)

30 Monday

🕐	What	Where
To do		

1 Tuesday

🕐	What	Where
To do		

2 Wednesday

🕐	What	Where
To do		

3 Thursday

🕐	What	Where
To do		

4 Friday

🕐	What	Where
To do		

5 Saturday

6 Sunday   St Nicholas' Day (Christian)

Tip of the week

Revisit your learning and revision strategies for each of the end-of-semester exams. Think about what did work and what didn't. Discuss approaches with fellow students. For all of you, being confident about your approach will reduce exam nerves and improve your performance. Use **Planning Resource 5.3** to focus your thoughts.

7 **Monday**

🕐	What	Where
To do		

8 **Tuesday**   Bodhi Day/Rohatsu (Buddhist)

🕐	What	Where
To do		

9 **Wednesday**

🕐	What	Where
To do		

10 Thursday
Human Rights Day

🕐	What	Where
To do		

11 Friday
Hanukkah begins (Jewish)

🕐	What	Where
To do		

12 Saturday

13 Sunday

Tip of the week
Study alongside others. As well as helping your learning by discussing the course content, you can spur each other on with sympathy, humour and the promise of a drink or coffee after each working period.

14 Monday

🕐	What	Where
To do		

15 Tuesday

🕐	What	Where
To do		

16 Wednesday

🕐	What	Where
To do		

17 Thursday

🕐	What	Where
To do		

18 Friday

Hanukkah ends (Jewish)

🕐	What	Where
To do		

19 Saturday

20 Sunday

Tip of the week

If you are feeling pressured by assignment deadlines, physical exercise is great for removing the symptoms of stress – go for a walk, jog or swim or go to the gym or a fitness class. On your return, refocus your efforts on working towards the deadline.

Winter Solstice/Yule
(Pagan/Wicca)

21 Monday

🕐	What	Where
To do		

22 Tuesday

🕐	What	Where
To do		

23 Wednesday

🕐	What	Where
To do		

24 Thursday

Christmas Eve (Christian)

🕐	What	Where
To do		

25 Friday

Christmas Day (Christian)

🕐	What	Where
To do		

26 Saturday

Boxing Day

27 Sunday

 Tip of the week

By now, you deserve a break from your studies, but you'll need to use some of the vacation constructively – for creating and working to a revision timetable for post-break exams or doing preparatory reading for the next semester's topics or modules.

Monday	Tuesday	Wednesday
28	29	30
4	5	6
11	12	13
18	19	20
25	26	27

Thursday	Friday	Saturday/Sunday
31	1	2
		3
7	8	9
		10
14	15	16
		17
21	22	23
		24
28	29	30
		31

Things to do this month

At this time in the academic year you will probably be . . .

. . . candidly reappraising your academic strengths and weaknesses.

By now you will be aware of what learning at your next level involves and you may wish to make changes to your approach. Test yourself using the tool produced by Howard Gardner on multiple intelligences (see http://www.businessballs.com/howardgardnermultipleintelligences.htm) and reflect on how you process information.

. . . reviewing your situation.

Sometimes life can get in the way; things happen at personal and academic levels and these may impact negatively on your studies. If this seems to be the case for you, don't struggle on alone. Universities have a range of support services to help you through any immediate difficulty. Speak in confidence to your Adviser of Studies about such problems and follow through on advice about what action you should take.

. . . learning how to analyse different forms of data.

Is the information reliable? Can you evaluate their inaccuracies or errors? Consider whether appropriate statistical methods have been used and whether the underlying hypotheses are the right ones. Concentrate on how results of any tests have been interpreted to establish whether the conclusions reached are correct. Try converting data into alternative display formats to see whether different features become more evident when the presentation is altered.

. . . broadening your understanding of the wider field of your study.

Take time to read more widely in the professional press about issues related to your discipline. Weekly publications such as *New Scientist*, *Nature*, *The Spectator*, *Newsweek* and *The Economist* keep you abreast of topical issues and are available online or perhaps in hard copy in university and public libraries. As an enthusiast for your subject, you will deepen and broaden your understanding and analytical skills (**Planning Resource 3.3**).

. . . developing your academic understanding.

Collect your marked work and study corrections and feedback comments to derive the full benefit of the advice your tutors have provided. If there is anything you don't understand, then arrange to meet with the marker(s) to receive further explanation (see also **Planning Resource 3.8**). These initial submissions will help you to become aware of what is expected of you. Knowing what you have done well and what aspects you need to work on will provide you with a framework on which to structure future assessed work, whether written or oral.

. . . developing strategies for remembering information.

Work on memorising techniques for long-term learning by creating your own mnemonics, acronyms, rhymes and other fact association strategies to remember key information. List key definitions, formulae, key terms, dates, personalities or events fundamental to your course. Regularly test your ability to recall this information until you are confident you can do so under exam pressure.

. . . reviewing your own value system.

Reflect on how exposure to alternative viewpoints, new information and approaches in your university learning has influenced your values and opinions. As part of this process, you may find that you are now more conscious of formulating your ideas based on analytical appraisal of a number of viewpoints, or evidence. As you become more practised in thinking analytically as a student (see **Planning Resource 3.3**), you will also become more aware of using this skill in your personal life.

28 Monday

Boxing Day holiday

🕐	What	Where
To do		

29 Tuesday

🕐	What	Where
To do		

30 Wednesday

🕐	What	Where
To do		

31 Thursday

New Year's Eve

⏰	What	Where
To do		

1 Friday

New Year's Day

⏰	What	Where
To do		

2 Saturday

3 Sunday

Tip of the week

Think about how you might direct some of your earned income from vacation employment (or Christmas gift money) to buy necessary items at cheaper prices in the winter sales (see **Planning Resource 1.6**).

4 Monday

Bank Holiday (Scotland)

🕐	What	Where
To do		

Twelfth Night (Christian)
Birthday of Guru Gobind Singh (Sikh)

5 Tuesday

🕐	What	Where
To do		

6 Wednesday

Epiphany (Christian)

🕐	What	Where
To do		

7 Thursday

🕐	What	Where
To do		

8 Friday

🕐	What	Where
To do		

9 Saturday

10 Sunday Baptism of Christ (Christian)

Tip of the week

If one of your New Year resolutions was to be more organised, start doing something about it now. Plan ahead for assessed coursework and exams, by noting the dates on these diary pages and in **Planning Resources 2.1, 3.1 and 5.2**.

11 Monday

🕐	What	Where
To do		

12 Tuesday

🕐	What	Where
To do		

13 Wednesday

Maghi (Sikh)

🕐	What	Where
To do		

14 Thursday

🕐	What	Where
To do		

15 Friday

🕐	What	Where
To do		

16 Saturday

17 Sunday World Religion Day (Bahá'í)

💡 Tip of the week

How did you use your time last semester? Have you got a good balance between study and other aspects of your life? Good study habits can help with time management, freeing up time for other things. See **Planning Resource 2.2** for five top tips for working more efficiently.

18 Monday

🕐	What	Where
To do		

19 Tuesday

🕐	What	Where
To do		

20 Wednesday

🕐	What	Where
To do		

21 Thursday

🕐	What	Where
To do		

22 Friday

🕐	What	Where
To do		

23 Saturday

24 Sunday

Tip of the week

You will be at your most effective as a student at particular times of day specific to you. Exploit this by doing intensive learning activities at these good times, and, when you are at an energy low, carry out routine tasks such as writing up and filing your notes.

25 Monday
Burns' Night (Scotland)

⏰	What	Where
To do		

26 Tuesday

⏰	What	Where
To do		

27 Wednesday
Holocaust Memorial Day

⏰	What	Where
To do		

28 Thursday

🕐	What	Where
To do		

29 Friday

🕐	What	Where
To do		

30 Saturday

31 Sunday

Tip of the week

At the end of the semester, it is important to collect your assessed work, since this is usually annotated by the marker. It is vital that you read and learn from these feedback comments if you want to improve your understanding for future submissions and exams (see **Planning Resource 3.8**).

Monthly planner

Monday	Tuesday	Wednesday
1	2	3
8	9	10
15	16	17
22	23	24
1	2	3

Thursday	Friday	Saturday/Sunday
4	5	6
		7
11	12	13
		14
18	19	20
		21
25	26	27
		28
4	5	6
		7

Things to do this month

_____
_____
_____
_____
_____
_____
_____
_____
_____
_____
_____
_____
_____
_____
_____
_____
_____
_____
_____
_____
_____
_____
_____
_____
_____

At this time in the academic year you will probably be . . .

. . . working more closely with fellow students in formal groups.

Assessment can often involve group work. Learn to work as an effective team member so you can perform better in group assignments. At the outset, agree as a group on how to coordinate your activities to achieve the required outcome, for example, a presentation (see Planning Resource 7.8) or poster (see Planning Resource 7.9). A deeper understanding of team roles can help everyone to contribute successfully.

. . . expanding your circle of friends.

Consider joining clubs and societies within your university, even at this stage in the year, as these will give you a chance to meet with a fresh group of students with whom you share an interest. Take the chance to participate in sports and other leisure activities that would not be open to you elsewhere. Lists of clubs and societies will be available on your Students' Union website.

. . . ensuring that you don't lose track of your reference sources.

Develop a system when note-making for writing assignments that identifies when you have recorded material word-for-word from the text. For example, you could highlight or write direct quotations in a different colour. Always ensure that, in addition to the publication details, you write down the page number or URL of the quotation as you will need to give this if you use the quote in your text. This all helps avoid plagiarism (see Planning Resource 4.1).

. . . developing your awareness of the range of resources available.

Although online material is perceived as the 'quick' way to access information, don't overlook conventional resources such as books and hard-copy journals. In many respects, these are easier to browse and read than the limited single-screen access of electronic versions. Make a point of exploring the relevant shelves in your library; you may find resources that will set your work apart from that of your peers.

. . . learning how to deploy quotes and discuss the work of others.

Avoid using too many quotations in your writing. Over-quotation is a form of plagiarism, *even if the quotes are correctly cited and presented.* Instead, paraphrase the idea from the source and use this to support your analysis of the topic. This shows that you understand why a point is important and not simply that you've found a relevant quote (see Planning Resource 4.3).

. . . reflecting on your recent exam experience.

Critically appraise your revision effort, the success of your exam strategy and the quality of each answer you gave. In light of your mark(s), consider how you might improve your approach in future exams (see Planning Resource 5.5).

. . . reflecting on tutorial, practical and laboratory work.

Think about what has been covered in these learning activities and assess what you have learnt from working in a group, in a pair or as a team member. Consider how your debating, negotiating and problem-solving skills have developed and contributed to your learning. Think also about how your confidence in speaking in public is developing.

February 2021

1 Monday

🕐	What	Where
To do		

Candlemas/Presentation of Christ
in the Temple (Christian)

2 Tuesday

🕐	What	Where
To do		

3 Wednesday

🕐	What	Where
To do		

4 Thursday

🕐	What	Where
To do		

5 Friday

🕐	What	Where
To do		

6 Saturday

7 Sunday

Tip of the week

Keep asking yourself questions about topics you're studying (see **Planning Resource 2.4**) – this will help you think more deeply, even after you feel a matter is fundamentally resolved or you understand it well. All critical thinking (see **Planning Resource 3.3**) is the result of asking yourself questions.

8 Monday

🕐	What	Where
To do		

9 Tuesday

🕐	What	Where
To do		

10 Wednesday

🕐	What	Where
To do		

11 Thursday

🕐	What	Where
To do		

Chinese New Year
(Buddhist, Confucian/Daoist)

12 Friday

🕐	What	Where
To do		

St Valentine's Day
(Christian)

13 Saturday

14 Sunday

Tip of the week

When looking at course materials or reading matter, try to look beyond the superficial. Assess quality of content over presentation, and consider the aims and motivations of the author(s) as well as the source and context in which the piece was written.

15 Monday

Nirvana Day (Buddhist/Jain)

🕐	What	Where
To do		

16 Tuesday

Shrove Tuesday (Christian)

🕐	What	Where
To do		

Ash Wednesday (Christian)

17 Wednesday

🕐	What	Where
To do		

18 Thursday

🕐	What	Where
To do		

19 Friday

🕐	What	Where
To do		

20 Saturday

21 Sunday

💡 Tip of the week

We all want to do well, but doing your very best can take too much time – a commodity that should be carefully rationed so that all tasks are given their fair share. Spending time to achieve perfection on one task may mean that you have less time to achieve a good mark on your next task.

22 Monday

🕐	What	Where
To do		

23 Tuesday

🕐	What	Where
To do		

24 Wednesday

🕐	What	Where
To do		

25 Thursday

🕐	What	Where
To do		

26 Friday

Purim (Jewish)

🕐	What	Where
To do		

27 Saturday Magha Puja Day (Buddhist)

28 Sunday

💡 Tip of the week

Share ideas and discuss topics with other students – the act of explaining can help your understanding and imprint the knowledge in your brain. It can also reveal things you don't really know, even if you thought you did.

Monthly planner

Monday	Tuesday	Wednesday
1	2	3
8	9	10
15	16	17
22	23	24
29	30	31

Thursday	Friday	Saturday/Sunday
4	5	6
		7
11	12	13
		14
18	19	20
		21
25	26	27
		28
1	2	3
		4

Things to do this month

At this time in the academic year you will probably be . . .

. . . coming to the end of the teaching period.

Make sure that you have registered for the forthcoming exams (if that is how your university does things) and check out the dates, times and exam locations for all your subjects. Log all this information in this planner and think about how you can use the remainder of the study period most effectively.

. . . planning for a change in your routine.

Evolve a realistic plan of work using the revision timetable (**Planning Resources 5.1 and 5.2**) so that time does not drain away when classes draw to an end, and your days lose the structure that you have established over the year. Be realistic about the need to balance study periods with employment, time for relaxation and 'housekeeping'.

. . . following the recognised presentation conventions of your discipline.

Be guided by instructions in your course handbook on the accepted style of citation, or on presentation of figures and tables in your subject. Follow the style consistently throughout your work. If you have doubts about the precise style or arrangement of data in other formats, follow the models used in texts or journal articles from your subject area. This is also important in avoiding plagiarism.

. . . modelling your own academic writing on other sources.

Take advantage of having access to good models of academic writing and presentation of logical discussion in the set textbooks. Familiarise yourself with the fairly strict and discipline-specific discourse conventions found in such academic writing. Read these materials with an eye for how an argument is structured and how evidence is used by academic authors to support or refute viewpoints.

. . . constructing your final assignments.

Critically assess what you write in terms of structure and presentation (see **Planning Resources 4.6, 7.1–7.9**). Ensure that the introduction outlines your approach to the task, that the main body flows logically and that the conclusion summarises your thoughts effectively. Read your text aloud to check for grammatical or factual errors.

. . . facing up to exams.

Neutralise any potential panic by getting yourself organised as early as possible. Set out a realistic revision timetable based on information gleaned from past papers (ensuring that these reflect the current course content), the course handbook, structure of the course content and advice from lecturers. Work systematically so that you stay on top of the work and capitalise on your growing confidence.

. . . taking stock of your academic skills.

Review how your learning style has adjusted to meet university requirements, and the different skills that you have developed over the year, for example, critical thinking, time management, handling large amounts of information, and construction of evidence-based argument (**Planning Resource 6.2**). Consider how you will apply these skills in the exams and how they may be incorporated within your CV.

1 Monday

St David's Day (Christian)

🕐	What	Where
To do		

2 Tuesday

🕐	What	Where
To do		

3 Wednesday

🕐	What	Where
To do		

4 Thursday

🕐	What	Where
To do		

5 Friday

🕐	What	Where
To do		

6 Saturday

7 Sunday

Tip of the week

Divide large tasks. If you feel intimidated by the size of a job and this prevents you from starting it, break the task down to manageable, achievable chunks. Then, try to complete at least one part every day. This technique can apply to revision as well as coursework.

8 Monday

Commonwealth Day

🕐	What	Where
To do		

9 Tuesday

🕐	What	Where
To do		

10 Wednesday

Laylat al Miraj (Islam)

🕐	What	Where
To do		

11 Thursday

🕐	What	Where
To do		

12 Friday

🕐	What	Where
To do		

13 Saturday
Birthday of L. Ron Hubbard (Scientology)

14 Sunday
Mothering Sunday (Christian)

Tip of the week

Academically, things will be getting busy now, so keep an eye on tasks you have to do over the following weeks and months. Plan your time to fulfil all the assignments, practical, lab and tutorial work on target. Reduce your social commitments if necessary.

15 Monday

🕐	What	Where
To do		

16 Tuesday

🕐	What	Where
To do		

17 Wednesday

St Patrick's Day (Ireland)

🕐	What	Where
To do		

18 Thursday

🕐	What	Where
To do		

19 Friday

🕐	What	Where
To do		

Naw-Rúz/New Year (Bahá'í)
Vernal Equinox

20 Saturday

21 Sunday

💡 **Tip of the week**

When submitting coursework, ensure that it is properly proof-read and edited to improve your marks. Use the checklist provided in **Planning Resource 3.7** to do this in several 'sweeps' through your draft. **Planning Resources 3.5 and 4.2** might also be useful at this stage.

22 Monday

🕐	What	Where
To do		

23 Tuesday

🕐	What	Where
To do		

24 Wednesday

🕐	What	Where
To do		

25 Thursday

🕐	What	Where
To do		

26 Friday

🕐	What	Where
To do		

27 Saturday
Pesach/Passover begins (Jewish)

28 Sunday
Laylat al Bara'at (Islam)
British Summer Time (BST) begins
Palm Sunday (Christian)

Tip of the week

Regard your exams as a set of routine professional tasks that allow you to demonstrate your knowledge. Be methodical in planning and doing your revision. This helps create a positive mindset and will build your confidence. You will feel in control of your revision and also be less likely to 'run out of steam' before your exam schedule is over.

Monday	Tuesday	Wednesday
29	30	31
5	6	7
12	13	14
19	20	21
26	27	28

Thursday	Friday	Saturday/Sunday
1	2	3
		4
8	9	10
		11
15	16	17
		18
22	23	24
		25
29	30	1
		2

Things to do this month

At this time in the academic year you will probably be . . .

 . . . thinking about your subject choices for the next academic year.

Before the summer break arrives, arrange to meet with subject tutors, course directors or careers advisers to discuss your options for the next academic year. They can explain how subject choices will fit with your degree plans and career aspirations. Talk to students who have already done the course for a 'consumer' view.

 . . . needing to make time and space for yourself.

Accept that you may have to act in a focused, maybe even selfish, way in order to deal with forthcoming exams. Negotiate with those around you to ensure that you can work without distraction and with whatever measure of privacy or group support you wish. Explain the short-term pressures to friends and family and ask for their help (and understanding).

 . . . developing your ability to evaluate content effectively.

In preparation for revision, go through your notes to ensure that these reflect the relative importance of facts, including: cause and effect relationships; compare and contrast listings; problem–solution–evaluation analyses; evidence in support of various viewpoints; and references to key publications within topic areas (see also **Planning Resource 2.4**).

 . . . re-assessing how you learn best.

Take a quick online test to analyse your dominant learning style (e.g. http://www. vark-learn.com/the-vark-questionnaire/) and consider how this is reflected in the ways you study. Consider whether the style you have identified is compatible with the study methods you have used previously. Identify ways in which you could use a wider variety of learning methods to help you prepare for forthcoming exams.

 . . . deriving a revision resource from your assessed assignments.

Go over the assessed assignments for each module and 'map' the content as a list of headings – a key term for each paragraph and sub-points for the detail. Make modifications in response to any feedback comments. Retain this 'map' as a revision aid for that topic. While it is unlikely that an identical question would appear in an exam, the substance of the topic may contribute significantly in responding to different questions.

 . . . appraising questions from past papers.

Bearing in mind the relevant learning outcomes, deconstruct past question papers, identifying the topics covered and the way the questions are framed. Work with a friend on drafting outline answers and practising writing full answers against the clock. Compare and evaluate your respective responses and think about your exam strategy (**Planning Resource 5.3**). If your exams are online and no past papers are available, then get together with colleagues and create your own question/answer quizzes.

 . . . constructing your own framework of knowledge and understanding.

As you plan your revision, take some time to reflect on the content and concepts that underpin your course. Go back to the course outline and the learning outcomes in your course or module handbook and use these to construct an overview of the topics you have covered. This rounded appraisal will underpin your revision and help to improve your exam results (**Planning Resource 5.5**).

29 **Monday**   Hola Mohalla (Sikh)

🕐	What	Where
To do		

30 **Tuesday**

🕐	What	Where
To do		

31 **Wednesday**

🕐	What	Where
To do		

1 Thursday

🕐	What	Where
To do		

2 Friday

Good Friday (Christian)

🕐	What	Where
To do		

3 Saturday

4 Sunday

Pesach/Passover ends (Jewish)
Easter Day (Christian)

Tip of the week

Make your distilled revision notes visually attractive – that way they will probably be more memorable. Leave white space around lists or other important items of information. This helps you to highlight concepts and leaves space for later additions.

5 Monday

Easter Monday Bank Holiday UK
(except Scotland)

🕐	What	Where
To do		

6 Tuesday

🕐	What	Where
To do		

7 Wednesday

🕐	What	Where
To do		

8 Thursday

Yom HaShoah/Holocaust Memorial Day (Jewish)

🕐	What	Where
To do		

9 Friday

🕐	What	Where
To do		

10 Saturday

11 Sunday

Tip of the week

When beginning your revision, use the intended learning outcomes from your module handbook to check your progress. Mapping the outcomes against the content of lectures, tutorials and labs can help you to gain a deeper understanding and so enhance your revision (see **Planning Resource 2.3**).

12 Monday

Ramadan begins (Islam)

🕐	What	Where
To do		

13 Tuesday

Baisakhi/Vaisakhi (Sikh)

🕐	What	Where
To do		

14 Wednesday

🕐	What	Where
To do		

15 Thursday

Yom HaAtzma'ut (Jewish)

🕐	What	Where
To do		

16 Friday

🕐	What	Where
To do		

17 Saturday

18 Sunday

Tip of the week

When revising, draw on the ideas and opinions of your peers and tutors. Discussing topics, reviewing comments on your assignments and swapping memorisation strategies can be very fruitful, revealing a range of interpretations and tactics that you might not have thought about on your own (see **Planning Resource 2.3**).

19 Monday

🕐	What	Where
To do		

20 Tuesday

First Day of Ridván (Bahá'í)

🕐	What	Where
To do		

21 Wednesday

🕐	What	Where
To do		

22 Thursday

🕐	What	Where
To do		

23 Friday

St George's Day (Christian)

🕐	What	Where
To do		

24 Saturday

25 Sunday

Mahcvir Jayanti (Jain)

Tip of the week

In the run-up to exams, test yourself regularly to confirm what you have learned. Without reference to notes or textbooks, jot down the key points, lists, formulae and so on that you have recently been attempting to memorise (see **Planning Resources 5.3 and 5.5**).

Monthly planner

Monday	Tuesday	Wednesday
26	27	28
3	4	5
10	11	12
17	18	19
24	25	26

Thursday	Friday	Saturday/Sunday
29	30	1
		2
6	7	8
		9
13	14	15
		16
20	21	22
		23
27	28	29
		30

Things to do this month

At this time in the academic year you will probably be . . .

. . . tying off the 'loose ends'.

Ensure that you have returned all borrowed items to the library and have paid all money due to the university. Students with a record of 'bad debt' within the institution may find themselves debarred from facilities or even graduating until the debt is paid.

. . . anticipating the benefits of vacation work.

Find part-time or temporary work by visiting your careers service 'job shop', which may list vacation employment opportunities, and by looking at local papers for seasonal work. Bear in mind how different types of vacation job, including internships, will complement your CV as evidence of your skills, experience and work ethic.

. . . becoming very focused on exams and all that these imply.

Try to view exams as the culmination of the semester's or year's academic work and not as an isolated event. Build on the strengths you have developed and challenge yourself to convert weaker areas into strengths by reviewing staff feedback and assimilating the advice into your revision material and strategy.

. . . selecting suitable working locations for revising.

For revision purposes, some people prefer an empty desk and an uncluttered room, others may like background music or the collegiality of a university reading room. If other people's noise interrupts your train of thought, a solution might be to go to a quiet zone in the library or an empty seminar room where you can be alone. Another option might be the anonymity of a public library reading room.

. . . consolidating your learning.

Make a habit of checking through your personal specialist terms or formulae lists frequently (**Planning Resource 2.5**) and make a conscious effort to learn how to spell the more difficult words or manipulate formulae correctly. This is an indication of your command of your subject that will pay dividends when you need to work quickly in exams.

. . . distilling your revision to cue words.

Reduce key concepts in your notes to bullet points listed on small cards or Post-it stickers. Practise recalling these 'cues' in response to a set of potential exam questions that you have drawn from past papers or created for yourself. Your ability to jot down key points quickly as part of a plan will save you time, give your answer structure and most of all give you confidence in your ability to recall the essentials of the topic.

. . . planning your exam strategy.

Work out exactly how much time you can allocate to answering each element of the exam after you have deducted time for reading the paper, planning the answers and checking over your completed script (see **Planning Resource 5.3**). When you practise answers, stick strictly to this time limit to assess exactly how much you can write in this time. In this way you will manage your time better in the exam while gaining optimum marks from producing as full an answer as possible within that time limit.

26 Monday

🕐	What	Where
To do		

27 Tuesday

Theravada New Year (Buddhist)

🕐	What	Where
To do		

28 Wednesday

Ninth Day of Ridván (Bahá'í)

🕐	What	Where
To do		

29 Thursday

🕐	What	Where
To do		

30 Friday

Lag B'Omer (Jewish)

🕐	What	Where
To do		

1 Saturday

Beltane (Pagan)

2 Sunday

Last day of Ridván (Bahá'í)

Tip of the week

Ahead of the exam, calculate how much time you can spend on each section of the paper. Stick to this schedule so that you can optimise your marks across the whole paper and avoid giving one brilliant answer but very poor responses for the rest.

3 Monday

Early May Bank Holiday

🕐	What	Where
To do		

4 Tuesday

🕐	What	Where
To do		

5 Wednesday

🕐	What	Where
To do		

6 Thursday

🕐	What	Where
To do		

7 Friday

🕐	What	Where
To do		

8 Saturday   Laylat al Qadr (Islam)

9 Sunday

Tip of the week

When updating your CV for summer job applications, use **Planning Resources 6.1 and 6.4**. Consult your course handbook for references to transferable skills that might be relevant, including those enhanced by your extracurricular activities.

10 Monday
Shavuot/Feast of Weeks begins (Jewish)

🕐	What	Where
To do		

11 Tuesday

🕐	What	Where
To do		

12 Wednesday
Ramadan ends (Islam) Eid al Fitr begins (Islam)

🕐	What	Where
To do		

13 Thursday

🕐	What	Where
To do		

14 Friday

🕐	What	Where
To do		

15 Saturday

16 Sunday

Tip of the week

Anticipate rewarding yourself with some pleasure/leisure activities that do not involve studying – catching up with new films, reading the latest bestseller or participating in sporting activities that you may have missed out on over the semester or term.

17 Monday

🕐	What	Where
To do		

Shavuot/Feast of Weeks ends (Jewish)
Visakha Puja/Buddha Day (Buddhist)

18 Tuesday

🕐	What	Where
To do		

19 Wednesday

🕐	What	Where
To do		

20 Thursday

🕐	What	Where
To do		

21 Friday

🕐	What	Where
To do		

Declaration of the Báb
(Bahá'í)

22 Saturday

23 Sunday

Tip of the week

Reappraise the way you have spent money over the preceding semesters. Could you have been more prudent in how you spent your money? Look at the tips in **Planning Resource 1.6** to see whether you might be able to change your habits to save money.

24 Monday

🕐	What	Where
To do		

25 Tuesday

🕐	What	Where
To do		

26 Wednesday

🕐	What	Where
To do		

27 Thursday

🕐	What	Where
To do		

28 Friday

Ascension of Bahá'u'lláh (Bahá'í)

🕐	What	Where
To do		

29 Saturday

30 Sunday

Trinity Sunday (Christian)

💡 Tip of the week

As you prepare to leave university for the summer vacation, make sure you have updated your PDP and CV (**Planning Resources 6.1–6.4**) and that you have visited careers and study advisers so you can choose the best module options for the next academic year taking into consideration your academic or career goals.

Monthly planner

Monday	Tuesday	Wednesday
31	1	2
7	8	9
14	15	16
21	22	23
28	29	30

Thursday	Friday	Saturday/Sunday
3	4	5
		6
10	11	12
		13
17	18	19
		20
24	25	26
		27
1	2	3
		4

At this time in the academic year you will probably be . . .

. . . thinking about how to enhance your employability.

Explore what openings are available in your institution for internships, school liaison and peer-mentoring. As a 'seasoned' student, you have something to offer to others and the experience will enhance your PDP and CV (**Planning Resources 6.3 and 6.4**). If you would like to participate in any of these schemes in the next academic year, prepare to make an early application for one of these potentially restricted places.

. . . planning to boost your finances during the vacation.

If you are planning to get a job during the vacation, ensure you save part of your income for semester-time. Put a proportion of your earnings in an 'untouchable' account and, even when relatively well-off, don't be tempted to splash out on luxury items.

. . . continuing to develop wider knowledge of your subject.

Catch up on 'peripheral' reading round your subject area over the summer months. For example, in addition to reading some of the specialist weekly publications that cover topics in your field, you might be able to start on 'light' background reading if you can obtain next year's reading list in advance.

. . . finishing off a year of your course.

Think about what you have liked and disliked about the learning you have done over the year. Did you prefer theory to practice? Did you prefer more self-directed learning or a lecturer-directed structured approach? Did you favour certain topics and find you were not attracted to others? Take these feelings into account when firming up your selection of modules for the new academic year.

. . . academic 'housekeeping'.

Once the exams are over, revisit the notes and other source materials used in preparing assignments. Order and refine these as appropriate, then file alongside corresponding course material for reference later in your course. You may find these foundation notes a good reference for later modules.

. . . thinking positively about oral examinations (where appropriate).

Prepare for oral examinations in much the same way as you would for written exams, that is, by compiling possible questions and your response to them. With a friend or family member, practise giving answers orally so that you develop some experience in responding succinctly and accurately because, in the exam, you will have only a short time to give your answer.

. . . thinking about the future.

The vacation is a good time to take a long, detached view of your career and life plans. You may find that the tedium of a holiday job focuses your thoughts on a well-paid professional career, or that the different people you meet provide a new perspective on life and your ambitions.

31 Monday
Spring Bank Holiday

🕐	What	Where
To do		

1 Tuesday

🕐	What	Where
To do		

2 Wednesday

🕐	What	Where
To do		

3 Thursday

Corpus Christi (Christian)

🕐	What	Where
To do		

4 Friday

🕐	What	Where
To do		

5 Saturday   World Environment Day

6 Sunday

💡 Tip of the week

During the forthcoming vacation, try to arrange a period away from 'learning and earning'. Take some time out to relax and do some of the things that you enjoy but may have denied yourself during the recent period of intensive study and examination pressure.

7 Monday

🕐	What	Where	
To do			

8 Tuesday

🕐	What	Where	
To do			

9 Wednesday

🕐	What	Where	
To do			

10 Thursday

🕐	What	Where
To do		

11 Friday

🕐	What	Where
To do		

12 Saturday

13 Sunday

Tip of the week

If you find that you have resits, the first priority is to establish when and where these will take place and then to register for them immediately. Make travel and accommodation arrangements, if necessary. Also, ensure that you forward promptly any resit fee that may be required, otherwise you may not be permitted to take the resit(s).

14 Monday

🕐	What	Where
To do		

15 Tuesday

🕐	What	Where
To do		

16 Wednesday

Martyrdom of Guru Arjan Dev (Sikh)

🕐	What	Where
To do		

17 Thursday

🕐	What	Where
To do		

18 Friday

🕐	What	Where
To do		

19 Saturday

20 Sunday

Father's Day (Interfaith)
Pentecost (Christian)

Tip of the week

If you do have a resit, prepare for revision by ensuring that you have all the necessary material to hand. This needs to be well-organised – especially lecture notes and textbook information. Make sure you set up and keep to your revision timetable (Planning Resources 5.1 and 5.2).

21 Monday
Summer Solstice

🕐	What	Where
To do		

22 Tuesday
Litha (Wicca)

🕐	What	Where
To do		

23 Wednesday

🕐	What	Where
To do		

24 Thursday

🕐	What	Where
To do		

25 Friday

🕐	What	Where
To do		

26 Saturday

27 Sunday

💡 Tip of the week

Give some thought to what you want to achieve during the upcoming vacation period. Will this be a chance to rest from your studies or can you use the time to do some useful background reading? Could you take a break from academic life by spending time developing new skills in a vacation job that will earn you money to support yourself next academic year? The choices are yours.

Monthly planner

Monday	Tuesday	Wednesday
28	29	30
5	6	7
12	13	14
19	20	21
26	27	28

Thursday	Friday	Saturday/Sunday
1	2	3
		4
8	9	10
		11
15	16	17
		18
22	23	24
		25
29	30	31
		1

Things to do this month

At this time in the academic year you will probably be . . .

. . . reflecting on your examination results.

If you passed, well done: enjoy the rest of the vacation. If you failed and have a resit, go back to basics by making good use of your course handbook – this will help you find out about the structure of your exam and the content that will be covered. Use the intended learning outcomes of the course to gain an insight into what lecturers will be expecting of you in the exam.

. . . doing vacation work.

Learn from new experiences outside the university environment and critically assess how the company or organisation you are working for now or others in a similar field might offer a career opportunity in the longer term. Keep a note of any contacts you have made – they could act as referees in future.

. . . addressing aspects of your past exam performance.

Consider how your recent exam results impact on your ambitions. The level of pass may have ramifications for your progression to specific courses. Investigate what you need to achieve in the forthcoming academic year to offset any academic weaknesses (see **Planning Resources 3.5, 3.8 and 5.5**). A study adviser may be able to help you explore ways to improve your performance (see university website for contact details).

. . . continuing to study 'informally'.

Even when not formally studying, look out for relevant articles, television programmes and specialist websites as sources of 'top up' information that will have potential future use in your studies. Where appropriate, keep a note of the source and date in case you wish to reference this information in the future.

. . . thinking ahead to project-style coursework.

Take time to analyse potential topics for project-type assignments that you may be required to do in the next academic year. Use the 'slack' time over the summer weeks to do some preparatory research to help choose among topic options or to identify whether resources are available to support a project you might propose.

. . . preparing for resits (if applicable).

Register for, and attend, any resit support programme offered by your institution. This will give you the chance to review your exam technique and enable you to take a detached look at why you failed. Working collaboratively with others in the same position can have beneficial effects on your ability to deal with the exams successfully.

. . . asking yourself 'What next?'

Reflect on the high points and low points of the past academic year. Consider whether these might influence your decisions about future academic, social, financial and career choices. For example, would you find it useful to do a refresher maths course, study a language, go on an advanced IT training course or work on your academic writing (e.g. **Planning Resources 3.5, 3.7, 3.8, 7.3 and 7.4**)? Use the search facility on your university's home page to identify what might be available to you within your institution.

28 Monday

🕐	What	Where
To do		

29 Tuesday

Feast Day of St Peter and St Paul (Christian)

🕐	What	Where
To do		

30 Wednesday

🕐	What	Where
To do		

1 Thursday

🕐	What	Where
To do		

2 Friday

🕐	What	Where
To do		

3 Saturday

4 Sunday

💡 Tip of the week

If you have a choice in subjects for the next academic year, prepare ahead for a meeting with your academic adviser by considering the options carefully – for example, module choices, personal feelings about topics and degree routes.

5 Monday

🕐	What	Where
To do		

6 Tuesday

🕐	What	Where
To do		

7 Wednesday

🕐	What	Where
To do		

8 Thursday

🕐	What	Where
To do		

9 Friday

Martyrdom of the Báb (Baháʼí)

🕐	What	Where
To do		

10 Saturday

11 Sunday

World Population Day

Tip of the week

Catch up with friends and family or deal with routine chores that you've put off while studying, revising and taking exams. Even the routine can be pleasurable when other pressures are absent.

12 Monday

Bank Holiday (Northern Ireland)

🕐	What	Where
To do		

13 Tuesday

Obon/Ullambana begins (Buddhist)

🕐	What	Where
To do		

14 Wednesday

🕐	What	Where
To do		

15 Thursday
Obon/Ullambana ends (Buddhist)

🕐	What	Where
To do		

16 Friday

🕐	What	Where
To do		

17 Saturday

18 Sunday
Tish'a B'Av (Jewish)

Tip of the week
Are you being as 'green' as you could be? Could you save money as well as the planet? Check the tips in **Planning Resources 1.6 and 1.7** to see whether you could change your habits and help the environment while improving your budget.

19 Monday

Waqf al Arafa (Islam)

🕐	What	Where
To do		

20 Tuesday

Eid al Adha begins (Islam)

🕐	What	Where
To do		

21 Wednesday

🕐	What	Where
To do		

22 Thursday

🕐	What	Where
To do		

23 Friday

Eid al Adha ends (Islam)

🕐	What	Where
To do		

24 Saturday
Asalha Puja Day (Buddhist)

25 Sunday

Tip of the week

If you have any resits, consider the revision and exam strategies that you adopted for earlier attempts. Could these have contributed to your lack of success? Think about amending your revision strategies and exam tactics in order to ensure that you do not follow an unsuccessful pattern again at the resits.

Monthly planner

Monday	Tuesday	Wednesday
26	27	28
2	3	4
9	10	11
16	17	18
23	24	25

Thursday	Friday	Saturday/Sunday
29	30	31
		1
5	6	7
		8
12	13	14
		15
19	20	21
		22
26	27	28
		29

Things to do this month

At this time in the academic year you will probably be . . .

. . . challenging yourself at the beginning of a new semester or term.

University is a time for taking up new or unusual interests – chances you may never have again. A new semester provides an opportunity to set yourself a fresh challenge for the year as a counter-balance to the intensity of your academic studies. For example, you might take up a new language, try sky-diving or take an advanced drivers' course, volunteer for a conservation project or aim to climb 20 Munros. Whatever your selected challenge, you will have found an outlet for your energy and enthusiasm that will bring you back refreshed for your studies.

. . . finding part-time work for semester/term time.

If you are on campus before most students arrive, then you can benefit from being first in line for any part-time work that might be available. Look at job adverts placed in Student Union buildings, job adverts in your university careers service or advertised weekly in local papers.

. . . preparing for the transition to your next year of study.

The transition from one year of study to the next is a good time to take stock of what you have achieved and of the challenges that you might have to confront as the work and what is expected of you increases. Think about new skills you may need to acquire or changes you may need to make in your study patterns and lifestyle to accommodate these.

. . . identifying the area of interest in which you might wish to specialise.

Some people come to university with a very clear idea of what they want to make their specialist study; others come to this decision after some time. It's not unusual for people's interests to change as they become engrossed in new areas of study. If this happens for you, make sure that you act by discussing possible module or degree changes with your study adviser or course director to ensure that you are following a programme of studies appropriate to your revised academic and career goals.

. . . thinking ahead to different styles of assessment.

Increasingly academics are introducing different modes of assessment. For example, you may be required to keep a learning log, a personal 'blog', participate in a formal debate or deliver a multimedia presentation. Have a look at what the requirements of your coursework for the next academic year will be so that, should you wish, you could try to do some preparatory reading. In addition, review your skills and consider taking a short course to develop those you might require. Often these are provided by academic skills tutors within your institution.

. . . receiving resit results (if relevant).

If you have done well, then you can look forward to your next academic year. If you have been less successful, then consult your study adviser, careers service or course director(s) about what options are open to you. University regulations may provide for different actions to allow you to continue your studies – for example, repeating the module again alongside next year's modules, repeating the year or changing courses.

. . . making your contribution to the student community.

As you prepare for the next stage in your academic career, reflect on what skills you are developing that will contribute to a good CV profile and think also about how you might develop these further, not only to your own advantage, but also to the advantage of the student community, for example, by participating in student representation as a class rep or standing for a position within your Students' Union or Association.

26 Monday

🕐	What	Where
To do		

27 Tuesday

🕐	What	Where
To do		

28 Wednesday

🕐	What	Where
To do		

29 Thursday

🕐	What	Where
To do		

30 Friday

🕐	What	Where
To do		

31 Saturday

1 Sunday   Lammas (Christian/Pagan)

💡 Tip of the week

Try to prepare yourself for the resit exam day by drawing up practice answer plans for questions asked in previous papers. Alternatively, practise a past paper question within the same time that you would be able to allocate to it in the exam. This gives you a better idea of how much you can achieve and write in limited time.

2 Monday

Summer Bank Holiday (Scotland)

🕐	What	Where
To do		

3 Tuesday

🕐	What	Where
To do		

4 Wednesday

🕐	What	Where
To do		

5 Thursday

🕐	What	Where
To do		

6 Friday

🕐	What	Where
To do		

7 Saturday

8 Sunday

Tip of the week

If you have resits, focus your answers on providing evidence of deeper thinking as well as the basic facts and information – this will help you gain better grades, especially at higher levels of study. Aspects to consider are covered in **Planning Resources 3.3–3.5 and 5.5**.

9 **Monday**

🕐	What	Where
To do		

10 **Tuesday**   Al-Hijra/New Year (Islam)

🕐	What	Where
To do		

11 **Wednesday**

🕐	What	Where
To do		

12 Thursday

🕐	What	Where
To do		

13 Friday

🕐	What	Where
To do		

14 Saturday

15 Sunday

💡 Tip of the week

Look ahead to the new semester, find out about in-course assessments and how they will contribute to your module or degree grade. Performing well in these tasks is a good way of ensuring that you create a strong platform for the degree exams. Review strategies that you might need to develop for non-traditional assessment modes.

16 Monday

🕐	What	Where
To do		

17 Tuesday

🕐	What	Where
To do		

18 Wednesday

Ashura (Islam)

🕐	What	Where
To do		

19 Thursday

🕐	What	Where
To do		

20 Friday

🕐	What	Where
To do		

21 Saturday Raksha Bandhan (Hindu)   ## 22 Sunday

Tip of the week

Reflect on your planning activities for the past year. Has keeping a note of forthcoming activities and deadlines been helpful? Have you benefitted from making 'to do' lists? Have the tips in this planner been timely and useful? If so, then you might consider purchasing the 2021–2 edition, available online and at your local bookseller.

23 Monday

🕐	What	Where
To do		

24 Tuesday

🕐	What	Where
To do		

25 Wednesday

🕐	What	Where
To do		

26 Thursday

🕐	What	Where
To do		

27 Friday

🕐	What	Where
To do		

28 Saturday

29 Sunday

Krishna Janmashtami
(Hindu)

💡 Tip of the week

If you have found the tips and planning resources in this publication useful, you might consider purchasing one of the more detailed books on which they are based. *The Study Skills Book* covers the full spectrum of undergraduate skills, while other companion volumes in the series cover more specific areas, such as essays and assignments, critical thinking, numeracy and project work. They are designed to help you with the future academic challenges you will face. For details, consult page 268 and www.pearsoned.co.uk/studyskills

PLANNING RESOURCES:
Developing your organisational and study skills

Planning resources: developing your organisational and study skills

All the material in this Planning Resources *section is copyright free and may be photocopied for personal use.*

1.1 Checklist of items you may require in preparation for the start of the new term

Especially if you are leaving home to go to university, you will need a good packing list. This should include:

- ❑ University literature, e.g. course information received
- ❑ Financial details for fees/loan/rent
- ❑ Academic books or e-books from recommended reading list
- ❑ Computer/laptop/tablet
- ❑ Chargers and adaptors as appropriate
- ❑ Stationery items e.g. files/folders/specialist lab books
- ❑ Secure storage for legal documents

- ❑ Driving licence/passport/ID, e.g. birth certificate
- ❑ Insurance details – personal/car/belongings
- ❑ Bank account details/bank cards as appropriate
- ❑ Clothing (for all weather conditions/activities/field trips)
- ❑ Cooking equipment (with recipes, if required)
- ❑ Bedding (if required)
- ❑ Study lamp (as necessary)

Further information about preparing for university can be found in relevant chapters within **The Study Skills Book**

1.2 Checklist of aspects to consider in relation to rented accommodation

Some compromise will almost certainly be necessary, so it might be a good idea to weight each aspect (e.g. by giving them an importance rating out of 10), then consider how each accommodation option matches these weightings.

- ❑ Rental cost
- ❑ Room size
- ❑ Single or shared room
- ❑ En-suite bathroom or shared facilities
- ❑ Comfort rating (heating, furniture, bed)
- ❑ Whether meals are included/standard of kitchen facilities

- ❑ Charges for internet connection/phone line
- ❑ Study facilities
- ❑ Distance from campus and lecture halls
- ❑ Travel implications/parking costs
- ❑ Nearby social, sporting and other amenities
- ❑ Social mix of the area

Further points about accommodation can be found in relevant chapters within **The Study Skills Book**

1.3 Planning your finances as a student

Keeping to a budget is one of the hardest parts of student life. This list provides tips for managing your money, keeping costs down and making the most of vacation earnings.

Budget smart

→ Create a budget spreadsheet.

→ Actively monitor your weekly or monthly expenditure.

→ Keep updating your budget figures so you are in control of your finances.

→ Keep some money back for known future costs as well as for contingencies.

Bank smart

→ Check out the best deals in bank and building society accounts.

→ Consider applying for an account with reward features for deposits and outgoings.

→ Keep track of your account balance.

→ At the start of semester put loan or other income into an interest-bearing account.

→ Move your debt if necessary. Credit cards differ greatly in interest rate and may have good introductory deals.

Shop smart

→ Shop around and look for special deals.

→ Join your favourite supermarket's loyalty scheme so you can benefit from points gained by shopping.

→ Try not to use store credit cards as they generally have very high interest rates unless you pay off the entire balance each month.

→ Play supermarkets at their own game: choose the location, time and place to buy your food.

→ Save on insurance costs by shopping around when looking for insurance cover.

Earn smart

→ Put a proportion of your vacation earnings in an 'untouchable' account to cover your expenses for term-time.

→ Take full advantage of 'perks' of the job, such as free meals or cheap goods.

→ Save any tips separately for a treat or special item.

→ Ensure you aren't being taxed at an inappropriate 'emergency' rate: contact your local tax office if unsure, quoting your National Insurance (NI) number.

→ When in funds, don't be tempted to splash out on luxuries you don't really need.

Further guidance on financial and budgeting issues can be found in relevant chapters within **The Study Skills Book**

1.4 Budget spreadsheet for student income and expenditure

Fill in the income and expenditure estimates for your budget, entering yearly, monthly or weekly components as convenient, then scaling up or down to fill the other columns. Total the yearly column, then work out the projected balance over the whole year.

	Predicted income		
Income	Yearly total (£)	Monthly total (£)	Weekly total (£)
Parental allowance/family income			
Part-time employment			
Child benefit/tax credits/other state benefits			
From savings (interest or capital)			
Scholarships and grants			
Loan:			
Loan:			
Other:			
Other:			
Other:			
Other:			
Total predicted income			

Expenditure	Predicted expenditure		
	Yearly total (£)	Monthly total (£)	Weekly total (£)
Tuition fees (as applicable)			
Books and other course equipment and supplies			
Annual membership fees (e.g. clubs, societies)			
Accommodation (rent, mortgage)			
Home and contents insurance			
Utilities (e.g. electricity, gas)			
Communications (mobile, landline, wifi, internet)			
TV licence and satellite/cable fees			
Credit card/loan repayments			
Transport costs			
Food and drink			
Clothing and laundry			
Childcare			
Health (including optician, dentist, prescriptions)			
Leisure and entertainment			
Holidays, including insurance			
Presents			
Allowance for emergencies			
Miscellaneous (e.g. haircuts)			
Other:			
Total predicted expenditure			

Projected balance: predicted income minus predicted expenditure over whole year

*Further points about balancing a budget while at university can be found in relevant chapters within **The Study Skills Book***

1.5 Planning your learning approach for the new academic year

Think about the changes you have made and challenges you have successfully faced to get to this stage. Use this as a positive springboard to organise and plan your learning.

Looking ahead

→ Review your long-term goals and reappraise them if necessary.

→ Prepare mentally for the autonomous, self-directed learning required at university.

→ Speak to advisers about your study and career options.

Participating

→ Sign up for an activity that's fresh and new for you.

→ Choose to get to know a new group of fellow students.

→ Get involved in student representation.

→ Study on campus rather than in your house or room.

Making sure you are in control

→ Prepare well for lectures and other learning activities.

→ Resolve to keep your paperwork in good order.

→ Decide to organise your activities and time as effectively as possible.

→ Get into the habit of using this diary/planner to note significant dates/times.

→ Use 'to do' lists to note and prioritise your activities.

→ Make sure you keep your finances in order by creating and sticking to a budget.

Making the most of learning opportunities

→ Start with an open mind and learn to think for yourself.

→ Keep up with the work.

→ Study regularly right from the start.

→ Speak to academic staff, tutors and advisers if you are having difficulty with subject material from your course.

→ Study collaboratively with your fellow students.

→ Find out about the assessment methods used on your course. Tailor your approach to study taking these into account. These approaches may vary from subject to subject.

→ If in doubt about any aspect of your learning, always make sure you ask!

*Further points in the chapters about understanding what university involves can be found within **The Study Skills Book***

1.6 Thrifty tips for money-wise students

Saving yourself money is always a good idea but it does not mean that you have to be uncomfortable to achieve this. Most of the following tips have the advantage of helping you to cut costs while improving your lifestyle.

Cooking economically

→ Cook from raw ingredients – healthier (usually less salt, fat, sugar) and often just as fast as a ready meal. Fresh fruit and vegetables bought 'loose' rather than pre-packed are often cheaper.

→ Cook multi-meals – if you cook double amounts of food in one go, then you will save fuel costs by working on the principle of 'eat one, freeze one'.

→ Cook for the flat – if you are living in a flat, then negotiate a cooking 'rota' so that you achieve economies by cooking the same thing for everyone. This saves fuel and gives everyone a chance to contribute. Be aware that this may take some negotiation to find dishes that everyone likes; also you may need to take into account that some people are subject to allergic reactions to some foods, e.g. nuts, dairy products and wheat.

Shopping cost-effectively

→ Shop when you have already eaten – people tend to buy more food than they actually need when they are hungry.

→ Use a shopping list. Make a list of what you actually require; offers can tempt you to buy things that you may not really need and that only save you a few pence.

→ Try doing food shopping online – sometimes this can take away the temptation of buying offers that you don't need.

→ Shop around for best prices – do price comparisons and buy where the price is cheapest not simply where the shop is convenient. However, balance out the time it will take you to go somewhere else and whether travel costs might cancel out any savings on your purchases.

→ Register for supermarket loyalty cards – these can sometimes offer special student deals but ensure that you can redeem saved points in other branches. Conversely, when you do see a good deal or offer, then arrange to split the cost with a friend.

→ Perhaps along with friends, consider bulk-buying if this will result in a saving.

→ Use cash-off vouchers – but only if you actually need the item.

→ Browse in charity shops – apart from offering items for sale that are cheaper in price, your custom allows the charity to further its cause.

→ Look out for 'freecycle' organisations – these can be found online and often exist locally. This mutual help system allows you to pick up things that are second-hand but serviceable and that would cost a considerable amount to buy new.

→ Spend wisely – consider buying new, better-quality items since generally these last longer than cheaper options; you need to make a judgement about how much use you will require of the item and how long you will need it.

Stationery savings

→ Use both sides of paper; use draft printing option where feasible.

→ Take notes electronically, but be sure to back up what you have recorded.

→ Use recycled paper for printing wherever possible (but make sure that cheaper recycled paper won't create difficulties with your printer).

→ Note that recycled ink cartridges can clog up your printer and may not last as long as the proprietary brand. They may be a false economy; you need to experiment to see which offers better value.

→ Shop around to find a company or group that will print final projects most cheaply.

→ Save postal charges and cost of greetings cards by sending e-greetings.

→ Re-use envelopes by using adhesive labels on a previously used envelope.

Travel reductions

→ Look out for student discounts, travel card deals, cheap rate travel periods and other offers that may be seasonal. Travelling by some forms of public transport is generally more expensive at peak periods.

→ Remember that walking is free and fitness follows! Cycling is another cheap option.

Do it yourself

→ Learn to bake and cook for yourself – often cheaper and more nutritious than ready-meal food.

→ Learn how to bulk-freeze raw vegetables when in season.

→ If you have the facility, grow some of your own food.

Mend not spend

→ Darn, stitch, repair, take shoes to the mender.

→ Check trouble-shooting tips in user manuals when things break down or malfunction.

→ Often user manuals can be consulted online and some may be downloadable.

Further advice on being money-wise can be found in the chapter on budgeting in **The Study Skills Book**

1.7 The green student profile

Deciding to make your contribution to improving the environment is regarded by many as a social responsibility. As the following tips illustrate, in ways that are undemanding, various organisations, including universities, have taken initiatives to assist you to make your contribution to promoting a 'greener' way of life and environment. For other aspects, you can act individually to save yourself money and protect the world's resources.

Find out about local authority and charity initiatives

→ Recycling centres and points – find out where your nearest recycling points are and what you can deposit there. Typical items include: aluminium cans (flattened); small batteries, car batteries; cardboard; clothing; curtains; fluorescent light strips; tins; fridges and freezers; glass; IT (computing) appliances; newspapers; oil (cooking, mineral, engine); paper; plastic (see symbols for possibilities); rags; tyres; vegetable peelings; wood.

→ Recycling rota – find out from your landlord or local authority what the schedule of collection of recycled items is for your street/area and which bins to use.

→ Charities and recycling – some accept ink cartridges; mobile phones; Christmas and greetings cards; used postage stamps (enquire at charity shops for possibilities).

Energy-saving initiatives

→ Save on fuel: heating costs can be reduced by turning central heating down a couple of degrees; switch off appliances rather than leaving on standby; turn out lights when a room is not in use.

→ Sell unwanted goods on internet auction sites or at car boot sales; alternatively join a 'freecycle' scheme to exchange unwanted second-hand items without a money transaction being involved.

Paper-saving initiatives

→ Reject unwanted mail – register with the Mailing Preference Service (information online) to stop unwanted junk mail being delivered to your address.

Repairing, conserving and re-using items

→ Use empty yoghurt cartons and other food containers for freezing small quantities of excess food.

→ Use rechargeable batteries and energy-saving light bulbs, where practical.

→ Buying items 'loose' or measured to your requirements rather than in pre-packed units will allow you to buy what you actually need rather than being left with extra material you may never use.

→ Consider re-purposing unwanted clothes by donating to your preferred charities.

2.1 Organising your personal coursework deadlines

Use the tables below to note all coursework deadlines and assessment dates. This information should be sourced from handbooks and your virtual learning environment (VLE) as soon as possible in the semester/term. Add the deadlines to the diary and planner sections. Now work back considering the different phases of assignment completion (see **Planning Resource 3.1**) to give a series of mileposts in your diary/planner.

Subject and topic	Deadline	Notes

Subject and topic	Deadline	Notes

Subject and topic	Deadline	Notes

*Further points about planning coursework assignments can be found in relevant chapters within **The Study Skills Book***

2.2 Good time management for studying

Managing your time effectively is an important key to success at university. These five top tips can help you to achieve this goal.

1. Do important work when you are at your most productive.
2. Make the most of small scraps of time, but factor in leisure and relaxation.
3. Keep your documents organised.
4. Make sure you always have a plan and work to it.
5. Extend your working day.

2.3 Planning your self-directed learning at university

At university it's up to you when you study beyond fixed lectures, tutorials, laboratory sessions and other practical activities. These tips suggest some ways in which you can use this time and your effort as productively as possible and so become an independent learner.

→ **Know your best time to study.** You are at your most effective as a student at particular times of day so exploit this by doing intensive learning activities at these times.

→ **Check out the hours that facilities are open.** Find out the library, study centre or computing facility opening times. Plan your study periods around those if you prefer studying in these settings.

→ **Plan ahead.** Keep an eye on things you have to do over the following week/month and plan your time to fulfil all the assignments, lab and tutorial work on time.

→ **Develop a personal filing system.** Learn to be methodical in the way that you store notes, handouts and any other printed materials within your filing system.

→ **Think about the underlying principles involved in your learning.** Keep your focus on the bigger picture and avoid becoming bogged down in the minutiae.

→ **Take breaks.** When working on your own it is essential to take breaks. It is important to maintain your social networks and taking regular short breaks with fellow students helps you to maintain a healthy perspective on your work.

→ **Work with a buddy.** Although studying is something that you need to do primarily on your own, coming together with others on your course to compare notes, confirm understanding of more difficult points and discuss a set assignment can help the learning of all involved. This contributes to the consolidation of your learning and helps identify gaps in your knowledge.

→ **Develop your professional vocabulary.** For subject-specific and general language, it will help you to remember words if you write them down along with a simple definition. (See **Planning Resource 2.5**.)

→ **Reinforce your learning.** You will need to be able to use the language of your subject appropriately and make sure terms are spelt correctly; you may need to master key formulae so that they become second nature to you. This is a reflection on your command of your subject. Make a habit of checking through your glossary or formulae lists frequently so that you can make a conscious effort to learn how to spell the more difficult words or lay out formulae accurately.

→ **Tackle tutorial questions.** If your course requires you to complete any sort of preliminary questions in preparation, then do the full set of tutorial questions, even when you don't have to submit them (they may reappear in exams). Check your answers from the answer key, if provided. If you have difficulty in working out a particular solution, then ask one of your lecturers or tutors to give you some guidance. Once you are satisfied that you have the correct answers, file the tutorial sheets alongside the related topic notes.

→ **Go through your module/course/departmental handbook.** Note down all the relevant topic areas that will be covered on your course. Use these topics as headings for the dividers for your files so that you have an allocated space for the notes when you receive them or compile them for yourself.

→ **Visit your subject department/school.** Find out where the noticeboard for your year is situated; visit the online home pages to find out if there is any special area that provides routinely updated information for students; visit your virtual learning environment and explore any sites that have been set up to support your learning. Familiarising yourself with where to find information at an early stage in the course will save you a lot of time later when you are under greater pressure.

→ **Review your skills and learning patterns.** If you are 'rusty' on word-processing or not quite sure of how to search a resource database such as a library catalogue, then make it a priority to upgrade your skills. You can do this by consulting the appropriate facility or service in your university to access an induction or training course.

Further points about studying independently for university can be found in relevant chapters within **The Study Skills Book**

2.4 Smart questions to ask yourself as you study
Sometimes you become so wrapped up in the mechanics of a task like note-taking or reading a text that you may not think about the deeper aspects or the wider view. Use this list of questions to help you to think more deeply about your learning.

Taking notes from lectures
→ What ideas were presented by the lecturer and why are they important?

→ Do I need to reorganise these notes to create a more logical sequence?

→ Is rewriting notes taking up too much of my time? Should I try to write my original notes more neatly if the only reason for rewriting them is to make them legible?

→ When I rewrite notes to help me to learn, could I synthesise the notes into bulleted lists, flow charts or diagrams rather than lengthy sentences?

→ Could I produce better notes by taking notes electronically in the lecture?

Making notes from texts

→ How is the information organised in the text?

→ How can I identify the key ideas quickly to provide an overview?

→ How best can I restructure the information into concise easily learned notes?

→ How much detail do I need to note for (a) learning about the topic, (b) eliciting information for an assignment, (c) revising for exams?

→ Have I noted key information about the source to be able to cite it appropriately (see **Planning Resources 4.4 and 4.5**)?

E-learning

→ Have I explored all the different features of the online learning environment?

→ Have I established a routine for frequently visiting the online learning environment, e.g. to check for new announcements?

→ Have I got a reliable system for filing e-materials, organising my bookmarks and backing up my files?

→ Am I taking part as much as I should in online discussions?

Thinking and reflecting

→ What are my own thoughts in relation to this topic?

→ What do I need to know – information or concepts (or both)?

→ How good is the evidence? What other evidence might be available? Where will I find this?

→ Are any patterns emerging from my study of the subject?

→ Am I thinking deeply enough about the material?

Doing examples and problems

→ Is the answer sensible, the working clearly presented and are the units correct?

→ Have I done what has been asked?

→ Is there anything else asked for?

→ Have I used the correct formulae?

→ Have I used all the information given?

→ How will this aspect of the course be examined?

Making the most of tutorials, lab and field work

→ Do I understand the aims of the session?

→ Have I done all the necessary background reading and preparation beforehand?

→ Have I thought about the session, and what I can learn from it?

→ For lab and field work, am I aware of any safety issues that might arise?

→ Am I ready and willing to participate fully?

*Further points about studying independently for university can be found in relevant chapters within **The Study Skills Book***

2.5 Keeping track of specialist terms and formulae

As you progress in your studies, you will be presented with new terminologies, new concepts and, depending on your discipline, new formulae and ways of applying logic to your analyses. It can take some time to come to terms with these new ways of expressing yourself or manipulating data and formulae. To help you with this initially as well as providing a memory aid for revision, you might wish to note down new terms or formulae in the boxes on this and the opposite page.

2.6 Instruction words commonly used for assignments and exams

The examples below are the product of research into the frequency of use of the most common exam instruction words. The definitions are suggestions; interpretation of the instruction is always context-specific. Using the list below will help you to provide the correct response to the task you have been set.

Instruction word	Definition – what you are expected to do
account [give an]	describe
account for	give reasons for
analyse	give an organised answer looking at all aspects
apply	put a theory into operation
assess	decide on value/importance
brief account [give a]	describe in a concise way
comment on	give your opinion
compare [with]	discuss similarities; draw conclusions on common areas
compile	make up [a list/plan/outline]
consider	describe/give your views on subject
contrast	discuss differences/draw own view
criticise	point out weak/strong points, i.e. balanced answer
define	give the meaning of a term concisely
demonstrate	show by example/evidence
describe	outline process/appearance/operation/sequence
devise	make up
discuss	give own thoughts and support your opinion or conclusion
evaluate	decide on merit of situation/argument

Instruction word	Definition – what you are expected to do
exemplify	show by giving examples
expand	give more information
explain how	describe how something works
identify	pinpoint/list
illustrate	give examples
indicate	point out, but not in great detail
integrate	bring together several concepts or points of view in a coherent account
interpret	explain meaning/significance by using examples/evidence and supporting views
justify	support the argument for . . .
list	make an organised list, e.g. events, process
outline	describe basic factors – limited information
plan	think how to organise something
report	make an account of process, event
review	write report – give facts and views on facts
show	demonstrate with supporting evidence
specify	give details of something
state	give a clear account of . . .
summarise	briefly give an account
trace	provide brief chronology of events/process
work out	find a solution, e.g. as in a maths problem

*Further advice about taking instruction words into account in answers can be found in relevant chapters within **The Study Skills Book***

2.7 Smart tips for effective learning online

E-learning is much more than simply accessing lecture notes and tutorial solutions in electronic formats; it can involve conducting online discussions, creating reflective learning logs and undertaking online assessments. Some of the required skills can easily be transferred, e.g. from experiences with social media, but in a university learning situation, a methodical and more reflective approach may be required. The following tips will help you to consolidate your learning by using online resources effectively.

→ **Take time at the start of each module to explore the online resources.** Although some features may not be activated immediately, it will be valuable to know the scope of the resource at your disposal and to consider this in relation to your assessment tasks.

→ **Get into a daily routine of visiting your Virtual Learning Environment (VLE).** There may be a convenient time at the start of the day or between lectures for you to look at emails and announcements. If you get into the habit of doing this on a daily basis, you won't miss important new information. Allocate some specific times to study online – your course outcomes may require a significant and ongoing input.

→ **Organise your online learning resources.** You could do this by grouping them within folders using the bookmark facility on your browser. This will keep the browser interface uncluttered and help you access the resources quickly, without having to remember or enter URLs.

→ **Be aware that staff may be monitoring your learning activities.** Although they may not contribute, staff may be able to see what you have written on discussion boards. They may also be able to interpret the number of times you have visited the VLE as an indicator of your participation in the course (although, generally speaking, if they are going to do this, they should tell you beforehand).

→ **Save on ink costs.** When printing out lecture notes based on PowerPoint presentations or similar, you may wish to select Pure Black and White from the colour/greyscale options on the print menu or you are liable to use up a lot of coloured ink printing the slide backgrounds.

→ **When consulting online resources, be aware that some material may not be of the standard or level you require** – too simple or too complex. This means you have to be selective in your source choices.

→ **When working online, be aware of the risks of plagiarism and copyright infringement.** **Planning Resources 4.1 and 4.2** explain plagiarism and provide tips on avoidance.

→ **Think about your approach to learning with online resources.** When using e-learning and fully online (e.g. distance learning) approaches, lecturers may make assumptions about the ways you are using the material. Make sure you understand what is expected of you. Also, check that you are using the material actively, that is, by engaging with the course content and recognising where topics appear in the syllabus, and taking part in activities that introduce and reinforce your learning (**Planning Resource 2.3** provides relevant tips).

→ **Research online learning support websites.** Take time to use a search engine to find websites that could be useful in your studies, such as: your university library website; textbook support websites; writing and study skills websites (often available within your own institution); sites related to specific course topics; and sites recommended by your tutors. Bookmark these and collate them in a folder.

Further points about using IT systems and VLEs can be found in relevant chapters within **The Study Skills Book**

3.1 Tool for planning the phases of assignment work

Tables like those that follow can aid you in organising the time and effort you put into coursework. They will help you balance effort among the component aspects and avoid rushing the job close to the submission deadline.

Task:

Date for completion: Date for submission:

Aspect of task	Time required	Target date for completion	Achieved
Analysing the task			
Doing preliminary reading			
Planning the response to the task			
Doing supplementary reading			
Writing the first draft			
Compiling a reference list in the recommended format			
Reviewing/amending the first draft			
Editing/proof-reading the final copy			
Printing/writing out the final copy			
Time margin for the unexpected			
Total time and final submission date			

Task:

Date for completion: Date for submission:

Aspect of task	Time required	Target date for completion	Achieved
Analysing the task			
Doing preliminary reading			
Planning the response to the task			
Doing supplementary reading			
Writing the first draft			
Compiling a reference list in the recommended format			
Reviewing/amending the first draft			
Editing/proof-reading the final copy			
Printing/writing out the final copy			
Time margin for the unexpected			
Total time and final submission date			

Task:

Date for completion: Date for submission:

Aspect of task	Time required	Target date for completion	Achieved
Analysing the task			
Doing preliminary reading			
Planning the response to the task			
Doing supplementary reading			
Writing the first draft			
Compiling a reference list in the recommended format			
Reviewing/amending the first draft			
Editing/proof-reading the final copy			
Printing/writing out the final copy			
Time margin for the unexpected			
Total time and final submission date			

✎ Task:

Date for completion: Date for submission:

Aspect of task	Time required	Target date for completion	Achieved
Analysing the task			
Doing preliminary reading			
Planning the response to the task			
Doing supplementary reading			
Writing the first draft			
Compiling a reference list in the recommended format			
Reviewing/amending the first draft			
Editing/proof-reading the final copy			
Printing/writing out the final copy			
Time margin for the unexpected			
Total time and final submission date			

3 | Planning and reviewing coursework assignments

✎ Task:

Date for completion: Date for submission:

Aspect of task	Time required	Target date for completion	Achieved
Analysing the task			
Doing preliminary reading			
Planning the response to the task			
Doing supplementary reading			
Writing the first draft			
Compiling a reference list in the recommended format			
Reviewing/amending the first draft			
Editing/proof-reading the final copy			
Printing/writing out the final copy			
Time margin for the unexpected			
Total time and final submission date			

*Further points about planning for assignments can be found in relevant chapters within **The Study Skills Book***

3.2 Tips for starting academic tasks and completing them on time

Two of the hardest parts of working on assignments are getting down to the work in the first place and completing tasks before the due date. The suggestions below will help you to begin in good time and complete your work promptly.

Improve your work environment
→ Tidy your desk before you start.

→ Reduce external noise.

→ Escape to a better location.

→ Avoid distractions.

Work effectively
→ Break up large tasks into smaller, achievable chunks.

→ Find a way to start, e.g. by general brainstorming of what you know (and don't know) about a topic.

→ Work in short bursts while your concentration is at a maximum.

→ Don't necessarily work in a linear fashion – work on sections out of sequence if you prefer.

Focus on the positive
→ Concentrate on things you do know, rather than those you don't.

→ Emphasise good results you want to tell people about, not efforts that failed to provide answers.

Get help from others
→ Work alongside fellow students.

→ Consult a fellow student, lecturer or skills adviser.

→ Visit one of the many websites that offer assistance, or consult academic support advisers on campus.

Don't be too much of a perfectionist
→ Perfectionism can prevent or delay you getting started. Your initial efforts don't need to be faultless. Less than ideal text can be refined later.

→ Achieving fault-free work requires progressively more effort, with less return as you get nearer to perfection; accept that you will have to 'draw a line' and submit the work for assessment, even if it is not as perfect as you would wish.

Further points about time management and overcoming writer's block can be found in relevant chapters within **The Study Skills Book**

3.3 Developing your critical thinking skills

University learning goes far beyond the simple memorisation of facts. As your learning and academic understanding develop, increasingly your tutors will suggest that you adopt a more questioning attitude in considering 'facts', issues and debates within your subject area. The following tips will assist you in becoming a deeper, more reflective learner. This critical thinking perspective should result in better grades.

→ **Focus on the task in hand.** It is very easy to become distracted when reading around a subject, or when discussing problems with others. Take care not to waste too much time on preliminaries and start relevant action as quickly as possible.

→ **Write down your thoughts.** The act of putting your thoughts into words is important as this forces you to clarify them. Also, since ideas are often fleeting, it makes sense to ensure you have a permanent record. Reviewing what you have written makes you more critical and can lead you on to new ideas.

→ **Be analytical, not descriptive.** Analysis is regarded as a higher-level skill than description in many disciplines. Most students lose marks because they simply quote facts or statements, without explaining their importance and context; that is, without showing their understanding of what the quote means or implies.

→ **Note appropriate citation information as you gather evidence.** The conventions for citation vary among subjects, so consult course handbooks or other information. Ensure you follow the instructions carefully, otherwise you may lose marks. **Planning Resource 4.2** provides tips on avoiding plagiarism.

→ **Draw on the ideas and opinions of your peers and tutors.** Discussions with others can be very fruitful, revealing a range of interpretations that you might not have thought about yourself. You may find it useful to bounce ideas off others. Tutors can provide useful guidance once you have done some reading.

→ **Keep an open mind.** Although you may start with preconceived ideas about a topic, you should try to be receptive to the ideas of others. You may find that your initial thoughts become altered by what you are reading and discussing. If there is not enough evidence to support any conclusion, be prepared to suspend judgement.

→ **Look beneath the surface.** Decide whether sources are dealing with facts or opinions; examine any assumptions made, including your own; think about the motivation of writers and the balance of evidence they cite. Rather than restating and describing your sources, focus on what they *mean* by what they write.

→ **Avoid common pitfalls of shallow thinking.** Try not to:

- rush to conclusions;
- generalise;
- oversimplify;
- personalise;
- use fallacious arguments;
- think in terms of stereotypes;
- make value judgements.

→ **Keep asking yourself questions.** A good way to think more deeply is to ask questions, even after you feel a matter is resolved or you understand it well. All critical thinking is the result of asking questions.

→ **Balance your arguments.** If asked to arrive at a position on a subject, you should try to do this in an even-handed way, by considering all possible viewpoints and by presenting your conclusion with supporting evidence.

→ **Practise looking for and examining different sides of an argument.** Choose a topic, perhaps one on which you have strong views (for example, a political matter, such as state support for private schooling; or an ethical one, such as the arguments for and against vivisection or abortion). Write down the supporting arguments for different sides of the issue, focusing on your least favoured option. This will help you see various sides of a debate as a matter of course.

→ **Analyse the instruction words in past exam papers and tutorial questions.** Note the types of instruction words commonly used. First, check that you understand what is expected in relation to each word (**Planning Resource 2.6** provides a list of instruction words and gives possible interpretations). Next, taking into account the subject and the way in which it has been taught, consider the level of thinking you are expected to demonstrate in your exam answers. If you are in doubt, ask a subject tutor to explain.

→ **Look into the murky world of fallacies and biased arguments.** There are some very good websites that provide lists of different types of these with examples. Investigate these using 'fallacy' or 'logical fallacies' in a search engine. Not only are the results quite entertaining at times, but you will find the knowledge obtained can help you to improve your analytical and debating skills.

Further points about thinking critically and evaluating information can be found in relevant chapters within **The Study Skills Book**. *A specialist text,* **How to Improve your Critical Thinking & Reflective Skills** *(see page 266) addresses these issues in detail.*

3.4 How to provide evidence of deeper thinking in your work

Assessment at university progressively demands deeper thinking about your subject, but many students are unsure of what is required. This list provides a practical set of tips that may direct your thinking appropriately.

1. Take time to consider and analyse the precise words used to describe the assignment, focusing particularly on the instruction word(s). **Planning Resource 2.6** provides a list of typical instruction words and their potential interpretation.

2. Make sure your response includes basic information and displays an understanding of it.

3. Supply additional relevant detail at the expected depth.

4. Be sure you understand what advanced thought processes are required.

5. Provide an analytical answer rather than descriptive one – focusing on deeper aspects of a topic, rather than merely recounting facts.

6. When planning your approach, use concept (mind) maps or grid layouts to ensure you consider different viewpoints and create a balanced review.

7. Set the problem or issue in context, and demonstrate a wider understanding of the topic. However, make sure you don't overdo this, or you may risk not answering the question/task set. For exams, remember that you cannot be expected to give the same amount of detail as you would in a piece of essay-style coursework or report.

8. Supply evidence of having read around the subject, by quoting relevant papers and reviews and stating authors' names and dates of publication. See **Planning Resource 4.3–4.5**.

9. Don't be afraid to question the views of researchers or commentators whose work you have read, but always support your viewpoint with evidence and logical argument.

10. Consider all sides of a topic/debate, and try to arrive at a clear conclusion, even if this is not decisive. You may have to take into account and explain two or more viewpoints, and possibly weigh them up, according to the task set. Where appropriate, your answer should demonstrate that you realise that the issue is complex and possibly unresolved.

*Further points about improving assessment and exam grades can be found in relevant chapters within **The Study Skills Book***

3.5 Common weaknesses in planning essay-style assignments

Despite having interesting and original ideas and approaches, many students do not achieve their potential because their written work is poorly structured. This list shows some of the common structural pitfalls and analyses how these can be avoided by planning your assignment carefully.

Symptom of weakness in structure	Analysis of the problem
The 'magical mystery tour' Answer rambles on, drifting from point to disconnected point with no real structure.	Essay may contain valuable content, but marks will be lost because this is not organised and the parts are not connected coherently.
No introduction and/or no conclusion Main body contains many useful points, but fails to introduce them and/or draw conclusions based on them.	Facts, concepts and ideas alone are not enough – evidence must be provided of deeper-level analytical thinking. The introduction and conclusions are important parts where this can be achieved.
The overly detailed answer Main body of the answer contains a wealth of information, some of which is relevant and some not. Little structure is evident and there is no discrimination between the important and the unimportant.	Writer preoccupied with showing how much has been researched/memorised, without showing how much has been understood. Relevance of the material has not been considered at the planning stage, nor as the essay-writing progresses. May lack critical analysis.
The 'stream of consciousness' Often written as if it were a conversational monologue, this lacks internal organisation, few (or too many) signposting words, no (or few) paragraphs, and little apparent logic.	Academic writing involves structural as well as linguistic components, both important elements of a good answer. Hence, the writing needs to guide the reader along a logical path to enable understanding. Irrelevant material should not be used as it will gain no marks and will waste time.
The waffly, irrelevant answer Fails to get to grips with the question and may contain large amounts of irrelevant information, without regard for the topic set.	Greater attention needs to be paid to analysis of the instruction given and converting these thoughts into a coherent answer plan. Irrelevant material should not be used as it will gain no marks.
The 'half-an-answer' Fails to recognise that there were two (or more) parts to the question. Focuses solely on one part, often the first part.	Answer should cover all aspects of the question as more marks may be allocated to the secondary part(s). This should be reflected in the answer plan and eventual structure.

continued

Symptom of weakness in structure	Analysis of the problem
Structure dominated by quotes Might start with a hackneyed quote or be interspersed with extensive quotes, with little effective use of these.	Such strategies leave little room for evidence of original thought. Few marks are given for repeating others – it's what is done with the information that counts.

Further points about writing essays and dissertations can be found in relevant chapters within **The Study Skills Book**

3.6 Typical elements of reports

When planning and writing reports, many students are unclear about what to include – this table provides possible elements and the expected content. Note that the elements defined here are listed in *alphabetical order* and not the order that they should appear in a report. Report formats differ and so not all elements will be included in the format required. You should always plan to adopt the precise format specified in your course handbook, or you will lose marks.

Element	Expected content
Abbreviations	A list of any abbreviations for technical terms used within the text (for example, DNA: deoxyribonucleic acid). These are also given within the text at the first point of use, for example '. . . deoxyribonucleic acid (DNA)'.
Abstract	A brief summary of the aims of the experiment or series of observations; the main outcomes (in words) and conclusions. This should allow someone to understand your main findings and what you think they mean. This is normally written last although it is usually positioned shortly after the title of the report.
Acknowledgements	A list of people who helped you, sometimes with a brief description of how.
Appendix (plural appendices)	Includes tabular information, usually, that only an expert would want or need to consult. A section where you can put items such as a questionnaire template, data or results that would otherwise disrupt the flow of the report or make the methods or results section too lengthy.
Bibliography/ References/ Literature cited	An alphabetical list of sources cited in the text, following one of the standard formats. In some disciplines, a bibliography is a list of all the reading done although not cited in the text. Check this out in your course handbook.

Element	Expected content
Discussion (or conclusions)	**Non-scientific-style reports:** In this section you might restate the problem or issue to be addressed (sometimes called 'the brief'), outline the key 'solutions' or responses to the problem, and explain the reason for favouring one over another by providing evidence to support that choice. In some, but not all, instances, a set of recommendations might be appropriate. **Scientific-style reports:** A commentary on the results and an outline of the main conclusions. This could include any or all of the following: • comments on the methods used; • mention of sources of errors; • conclusions from any statistical analysis; • comparison with other findings or the 'ideal' result; • what you think the results mean; • how you might improve the experiment(s); • how you might implement the findings (in a business report); • where you would go from here given more time and resources. Sometimes you might combine the results and discussion sections to allow a narrative to develop – to explain, for example, why one result led to the next experiment or approach. Be aware that a large proportion of marks may be given for your original thoughts in this section.
Executive summary	In a business report, this takes the place of an abstract. Gives the key points of the report, usually no more than one A4 page long. It should start with a brief statement of the aims of the report, a summary of the main findings and/or conclusions, perhaps given as bullet points, and a summary of the main conclusions and/or recommendations. You would normally write this part last although it is usually positioned shortly after the title of the report.
Experimental	A description of apparatus and method, similar to 'Materials and methods'.
Glossary	A list of terms that might be unfamiliar to the reader, with definitions.

continued

Element	Expected content
Introduction	**Non-scientific-style reports:** The context of the study and an outline of the problem or issue to be addressed, in other words, the aim of the report. This may require reference to the literature or other resource material to be used. **Scientific-style reports:** An outline of the background to the experiment or survey, the aims of the research and brief discussion of the techniques to be used. Your goal is to orientate the reader and explain what you have done and why.
Main body of text	This section includes your appraisal of the topic. It should systematically address solutions or issues in response to the report's purpose and provide an analysis of all pertinent matters. It may be subdivided into sections reflecting different aspects. In a scientific literature review, the approach is often to give a chronological account of developments in the field, quoting key authors and their ideas and findings. This section may include tables comparing different approaches or results in different studies. Figures tend to be rare but may be used to summarise concepts or illustrate key findings.
Materials and methods	A description of what was done. You should provide sufficient detail to allow a competent person to repeat the work.
Results	A description of the experiments/surveys carried out and the results obtained, usually presented in either tabular or graphic form (never both for the same data). You should point out meaningful aspects of the data, which need not be presented in the same order in which the work was done.
Table of contents	Effectively an outline list to allow the reader to find parts they are interested in reading more about. May also include a table of diagrams. More likely to be included in a lengthy report.
Title page	Full names of author(s), module title or code and the date. In a business report this may also include the company logo, client details, classification (for example, 'confidential'). **Non-scientific-style reports:** A concise but comprehensive title that defines the topic. **Scientific-style reports:** A descriptive title that indicates what was done, indicates any restrictions, and sometimes describes the 'headline' finding.

*Further points about report writing and the structure of different types of report can be found in relevant chapters within **The Study Skills Book***

3.7 Checklist for assignment presentation and editing

To achieve good grades, your assignment should reflect your knowledge and understanding. Thus, you need to plan, structure and present your work in the best way possible. For this reason, it is advisable to allocate time for reviewing your draft to ensure that you eliminate errors of content, expression, accuracy and presentation that may have been missed while you were creating the text. Each heading below represents a 'sweep' of the text, checking for the aspects shown. Experienced reviewers can accomplish all aspects at one reading, but you may find it easier to carry out a number of readings, paying attention to specific elements each time.

Content and relevance

❑ The intent of the instruction word has been followed (**Planning Resource 2.6** provides a sample list)

❑ The question or task has been completed, that is, you have answered all sections or required numbers of questions

❑ The structure is appropriate

❑ The text shows objectivity

❑ The examples are relevant

❑ All sources are acknowledged and correctly cited

❑ The facts presented are accurate

Clarity, style and coherence

❑ The aims and objectives are clear

❑ Clarity – what you wrote is what you meant

❑ Any informal language (including text abbreviations) has been removed

❑ The text is fluent, with appropriate use of signpost words and specialist terms

❑ The style is academic and appropriate for the task

❑ The content and style of each section is consistent

❑ The tense used in each section is suited to the time-frame within which you are writing

Grammatical correctness

- ❏ All sentences are complete
- ❏ All sentences make sense
- ❏ Paragraphs have been correctly constructed
- ❏ Suggestions made by grammar checker have been accepted/rejected
- ❏ The text has been checked against your own checklist of recurrent grammatical errors
- ❏ The text is consistent in adopting either British or American English usage

Spelling and punctuation

- ❏ Any blatant 'typos' have been corrected by reading for meaning
- ❏ The text has been spell-checked and any of your own most often misspelt words have been corrected
- ❏ A check has been made for spelling of subject-specific and non-English words
- ❏ Punctuation has been checked, if possible, by the 'reading aloud' method, i.e. inserting appropriate punctuation marks when a breathing pause is required or taken
- ❏ Proper names are correctly capitalised
- ❏ Overlong sentences have been divided

Presentation and coherence

- ❏ The text length meets word count target – neither too short, nor too long
- ❏ Overall neatness is acceptable
- ❏ The cover sheet details and presentation aspects are as required by your department
- ❏ The bibliography/reference list is correctly formatted
- ❏ Page numbers have been included (in position stipulated, if given)
- ❏ The figures and tables are in appropriate format and position

3.8 Common types of feedback comment and how to act in response

When providing feedback on your work, tutors may add comments as well as using the standard proof-reading symbols. Comments in the margin may be accompanied by underlining of word(s), circling of phrases, sentences or paragraphs. This table gives an indication of what the comment terms can be taken to mean in relation to (a) content, (b) structure and (c) presentation. Taking on board these pointers is an important way to develop your writing skills.

(A) CONTENT	
Type of comment and typical examples	**Meaning and potential remedial action**
Expressions of approval *Good!* *Excellent!* ✓ (may be repeated)	You got this right or chose a good example. Keep up the good work!
Specific factual comment or comment on your approach *You could have included . . .* *What about . . . ?* *Why didn't you . . . ?*	Depends on context, but it should be obvious what is required to accommodate the comment (if not, ask).
Relevance *Relevance?* *Importance?* *Value of example?* *So?*	An example or quotation may not be apt, or you may not have explained its relevance. Think about the logic of your narrative or argument and whether there is a mismatch as implied, or whether you could add further explanation; choose a more appropriate example or quote.
Detail *Give more information* *Example?* *Too much detail/waffle/padding*	You are expected to provide more detail or an example to illustrate your point; or you may have provided too much information. It may be that your work lacks substance and you appear to have compensated by putting in too much description rather than analysis, for example.
Expressions of disapproval *Poor/Weak* *? or !* (may be repeated)	Sometimes obvious, but may not be clear. The implication is that your examples, logic or expression could be improved. Ask for an explanation if unsure.

continued

(B) STRUCTURE	
Type of comment and typical examples	**Meaning and potential remedial action**
Failure to introduce topic clearly *Where are you going with this?*	What is your understanding of the task? What parameters will confine your response? How do you intend to tackle the subject?
Fault in logic or argument *Logic!* *Non sequitur* (does not follow)	Your argument or line of logic is faulty. This may require quite radical changes to your approach to the topic.
Failure to construct a logical discussion *Imbalanced discussion* *Weak on pros and cons*	When you have to compare and contrast in any way, then it is important that you give each element in your discussion equal coverage.
Heavy dependency on quotations *Watch out for over-quotation* *Too many quotations* *Over-quotation*	There is a real danger of plagiarism if you include too many direct quotations from text. You have to demonstrate that you can synthesise the information from sources as evidence of your understanding. However, in a subject such as English Literature or Law, quotation may be a key characteristic of writing. In this case, quotation is permitted, provided that it is supported by critical comment and correctly sourced.
Move text Loops and arrows (text) ⤳	Suggestion for changing order of text, usually to enhance the flow or logic.
Paragraph structure *N.P.* (for new paragraph), possibly with ⌐ symbol *Paragraphs!*	Paragraphs too long, leading to 'information overload' and failure to identify and separate out ideas or concepts to allow the reader to follow the thread and logic of your discussion.

(C) PRESENTATION

Type of comment and typical examples	Meaning and potential remedial action
Failure to follow recommended format *Please follow departmental template for reports*	If the department or school provides a template for the submission of reports, then you must follow it. There are good reasons, such as the need to follow professional conventions, especially in sciences. You must conform. If you don't, then you may lose marks.
Citations *Reference* *Reference required* *Reference list omitted* *References don't match citations in text*	You have not supported evidence, argument or a quotation with a reference to the original source. This is important in academic work, and if you fail to do it you may be considered guilty of plagiarism. If you omit to attach a reference list, this will lose you marks as it implies a totally unsourced piece of writing that suggests you have done no specialist reading. Citation and plagiarism are covered in relevant chapters of ***The Study Skills Book***.
Minor proofing errors Sp. Usually in margin (spelling) ⋏ Insert material here ⌐ Break paragraph here P Punctuation error ◡ Close up ℘ Delete (or ╱ or ⊢) (STET) Ignore marks (Latin for 'let it stand') ⟵ Run on ≡ Capital letter (or cap)	A (minor) correction is required. Although individually, these may indicate small errors, cumulatively they will create a negative impression of the quality and accuracy of your work.
Tidiness *Illegible!* *Untidy* *Can't read this*	(This may apply only to exam scripts.) Your handwriting may be difficult to decipher and you may be penalised (use a word processor, if allowed).

*Further points about reviewing, editing and responding positively to feedback can be found in relevant chapters within **The Study Skills Book***

Using source material responsibly: plagiarism, citation and referencing

4.1 Understanding the nature of plagiarism and the role of citation and referencing

The conventions of citation and referencing are used in academic work to acknowledge sources within your text. 'Citation' is when you use or paraphrase the work of others, while 'referencing' provides a signpost to the work that you've used so that readers can consult the source if they wish. Plagiarism occurs if a writer uses the work of others without acknowledging the source(s).

Academic plagiarism is a subtle and complex matter, perhaps best understood by considering examples. In a university context, the following actions would be regarded as plagiarism:

→ Copying and pasting sections of someone else's work into your own submission without acknowledging them.

→ Devoting more than 10% of your work to quotation.

→ Describing others' ideas – with or without quotation marks – without giving the source.

→ Using the work of others by keeping most of the words but rephrasing or substituting some alternatives and without acknowledgement of the source.

→ Copying material obtained from a fellow student and using it as your own.

→ Using the same material for more than one assignment.

→ Buying work from a commercial essay-writing company and submitting it as your own.

4.2 Smart tips for avoiding plagiarism

Intentional plagiarism can be detected through structural, presentational and linguistic analysis and many universities use sophisticated plagiarism detection software to confirm suggestions of plagiarism in someone's work. Penalties vary across courses and institutions. However, often plagiarism is unintentional; people can make genuine mistakes or may have misconceptions about the nature of plagiarism. In both instances, they may contravene plagiarism regulations.

The following tips should help you to avoid inadvertent plagiarism:

→ Learn how to cite and reference correctly and honourably to avoid the embarrassment and possible loss of marks or course credits.

→ Plan ahead by always noting down the publication details of sources you consult when researching for assignments. Organise all your sources into a list. If you do this systematically, when you are near to finishing your assignment you'll have all the information to hand and you will be able to refine the list to show only the relevant sources.

→ Double-check your departmental or university plagiarism policy. This should spell out the precise situations in which you might break rules. It may also give useful information on the department's preferred methods for citing sources.

→ Avoid copying material by electronic means. If you use the material in your work, then you must quote the source. If you fail to add an appropriate citation, this would be regarded as cheating.

→ Evaluate source material and identify your purpose in citing it. You need to be clear what the citation will do to complement the discussion in your work; if it adds nothing to the analysis or debate, then it should not be included.

→ Paraphrase the work you wish to cite. To do this, you need to take the essence of the idea and express it in your own words. If you simply take key phrases from the source material and rearrange them, or substitute some words with synonyms (words similar in meaning), this could be regarded as plagiarism.

→ Follow the academic convention of quoting sources. Even if you prefer to use your own wording rather than a direct copy of the original, you still need to cite the source. The reference to the source signifies that you are making that statement on the basis of the ideas reported there.

→ Double-check your 'original' ideas. If you have what you think is a novel idea, do not simply accept that your brainwave is unique. It is common for people to forget the original source of an idea that may resurface in their mind after many years and perhaps in a different context, and this may have happened to you. Think carefully about possible sources that you may have forgotten about; ask others (such as your tutor or supervisor) whether they have come across the idea before; and consult relevant texts, encyclopaedias or the internet.

→ Modify your note-making technique. You may risk plagiarising if you cannot recall or find the source of a piece of text. In your notes, put any direct transcriptions in quotes and add full details of the source whenever you take notes from a textbook or paper source. Always use quote marks ('…') when taking such notes *verbatim* from texts and other materials. This indicates that what you have written down is a direct copy of the words used, as you may forget this at a later time. You do not need to quote directly in the final version of your work, but can paraphrase the ideas.

→ Read the documentation about photocopying that is often available in the area around photocopying facilities. This will provide detailed information about current legislation and any local exceptions.

4.3 How to cite the work of others in your text

The point of citing someone's work is to support (or refute) a point you wish to make in your own text as part of your analysis. This shows critical thinking and respects the work of others that has shaped that thinking – whether positively or negatively.

→ **Author-prominent** (name of the author(s) integrated into the sentence), for example:

Cram (2018) holds the view that the language of text messaging has diminished writing and spelling skills across generations as evidenced in her research on adults aged 18 to 65 years.

→ **Information-prominent** (name of the author(s) in brackets at the end of the sentence), for example:

Writing and spelling skills have been diminished by texting language with its own specific discourse and abbreviations (Cram, 2018).

→ **Quotation in text.** Sometimes it is important to the thrust of your discussion to use the exact words from your source. This is done in one of two ways.

For 'short' quotes (fewer than 30 words) should be integrated within a sentence (note that quotations should not simply be inserted without explanation):

> Cram (2018) supports the case for a fresh approach to teaching literacy skills as 'writing and spelling skills …have diminished'.

For 'long' quotations (more than 30 words, although some systems specify 40 words or three or more lines of text), the quotation should be indented:

> In the last decade, at least, concern has been expressed by many researchers about a decline in literacy skills to the extent that
>
> > …adults aged 18-65 are demonstrating weaknesses in spelling, grammar and fluency in writing and our research has found this to be consistent over the age range and ability so that previously 'good' spellers and writers are finding their skills have diminished markedly (Cram, 2018:48).
>
> Where subjects reported a perception of diminished writing skills, they also found that their 'writing' was more likely to be done electronically rather than manually.

Note that the three dots known as 'ellipsis' (…) are used to show that some words have been omitted from the quotation, but without changing the sense of the quote (see 'short' quote example above). Ellipsis can also be used at the beginning of a quotation to link the quotation to the preceding sentence stem (as in the 'long' quotation example above).

4.4 How to create a reference list (bibliography)

To support the citations you have used in your text, you will need to provide a *reference list* of the sources. In some disciplines, you may be required to provide a *bibliography* which is the list of all the sources you used to research the topic but not cited in your text. In some cases, you may be required to provide both a reference list and a bibliography. Just to complicate things, some disciplines use the term 'bibliography' to cover the citations and the references used in a single list.

→ It is good practice when you begin reading or note-making from a source to note:

Source	Identifying information	Author(s)	Title	Publisher	Publication date	Place of publication
Books	Title, chapter, pages	Surname(s) + initials	In full	See title page	Plus edition if relevant	See page after title page
Journal	Title, volume number, issue, page(s)	As above	As above	As above	As above	
Website	URL	As above	As above	As above	May be in URL	

→ You will then need to use the above information in some permutation or other to compile your reference list/bibliography. *The precise style of doing this will depend on each subject you study*. Often such changes are driven by professional associations that have developed their singular styles, for example, the Modern Languages Association (MLA) and the American Psychological Association (APA). The main differences lie in the ordering and presentation of the information. Styles should not be mixed.

4.5 Examples of three common methods of citation and referencing

In all styles, the ordering and punctuation of the resources is important so that the information is presented consistently and accurately. For example, in some styles, for clarity, italicisation may be required for titles and for any Latin abbreviations used.

→ **Harvard style** (author name/date style)

Citation in text for a book:

> Cram (2018) holds the view that the language of text messaging has diminished writing and spelling skills across generations as evidenced in her research on adults aged 18 to 65 years.

In the reference list, for example:

> Cram, P., 2018. *The power of language: text messaging future for Generation Z*. London: Language Press.

→ **Modern Languages Association (MLA) style** (author name/page style)

In text (for a book) (number relates to the page number):

> Writing and spelling skills have been diminished by texting language with its own specific discourse and abbreviations (Cram 48).

In the reference list, for example:

> Cram, P., 2018. *The power of language: text messaging future for Generation Z*. London: Language Press.

→ **Vancouver style** (in-text numeric style)

In text (for a book) (number relates to number on reference list):

> Writing and spelling skills have been diminished by texting language with its own specific discourse and abbreviations (9).

In the reference list, for example:

> 9. Cram, P. *The power of language: text messaging future for Generation Z*. London: Language Press; 2018.

To demonstrate the styles, the above examples are confined to books. The many kinds of source material available mean that each of these styles has a layout approach that covers journal, electronic and media sources among others.

You may choose to use a software package to collate your reference list as you write your text. If you decide to follow that route, note that learning how to use the package may be counterproductive if balanced against the time that it would take you to compile the list manually yourself.

4.6 Abbreviations used in citations and references

While your course requires you to use one referencing style as standard, you will need to be able to understand what you read in material following other conventions. Common abbreviations used in some of the standard styles are given below

Term/Abbreviation	Full expression	Meaning
ch. or chs.	chapter/chapters	chapter
ed. or eds.	editor(s) or edition(s)	editor of a journal, book with several contributions
et al.	et alii	and others (for three or more authors)
ff.	foliis	following
ibid.	ibidem	in the same source as the previous item on the list
loc.cit.	loco citato	in the same place and page as previous same citation
op.cit.	opere citato	in the same place as a previously given source
passim	passim	throughout
p. or pp.	page/pages	
vide	vide	see (seek that word in a book or reference work)

Note that words and abbreviations in Latin should be placed in italics as non-English words. This information will help you to interpret the references more easily and accurately.

This section on plagiarism, citation and referencing presents a simplified outline of what is involved in following this potentially complex academic rules. While observing the rules, a mechanical exercise in many respects, your work will be devalued if you fail to follow whatever convention is appropriate to your university/school/course. Often, however, the course guidelines are not particularly detailed. You will find comprehensive methods, explanations and examples in *How to Cite, Reference & Avoid Plagiarism at University* by Kathleen McMillan and Jonathan Weyers (Pearson, 2013).

5.1 How to prepare a revision timetable

Having a plan can help you to feel more in control of your efforts and will help you to balance your time over different courses or topics (including the ones you consciously or unconsciously try to avoid). The sequence below is one effective way for setting up a revision timetable using a planning device like the one provided in **Planning Resource 5.2**.

1. Fix your exam schedule start and end dates.

2. Note down your essential non-study commitments.

3. Decide on the ideal number of 'sessions' you wish to study (by day and week).

4. Allocate these revision sessions to the different subjects or topics you need to cover.

5. In allocating time, recognise that you cannot work continuously if you want to study effectively. Make time for resting.

6. Programme revision slots for when you normally work most effectively, and other routine tasks when you tend not to be at your best.

7. Include some empty slots in your timetable to allow for unforeseen problems or changes in your plans.

8. If at all possible, try to ease back on your revision load near the exam.

*Further points about revision technique and timetabling can be found in relevant chapters within **The Study Skills Book***

5.2 Timetable templates for personal revision

These have been designed to help you organise your effort. **Planning Resource 5.1** provides tips for filling the templates in.

	Monday	Tuesday	Wednesday
Morning			
Lunch			
Afternoon			
Evening meal			
Evening			

Week:		Key to subjects/topics:	

Thursday	Friday	Saturday	Sunday

Week:	Key to subjects/topics:

	Monday	Tuesday	Wednesday
Morning			
Lunch			
Afternoon			
Evening meal			
Evening			

Thursday	Friday	Saturday	Sunday

5 Planning for exams

Week: **Key to subjects/topics:**

	Monday	Tuesday	Wednesday
Morning			
Lunch			
Afternoon			
Evening meal			
Evening			

Thursday	Friday	Saturday	Sunday

Week: **Key to subjects/topics:**

	Monday	Tuesday	Wednesday
Morning			
Lunch			
Afternoon			
Evening meal			
Evening			

Thursday	Friday	Saturday	Sunday

5.3 Essential questions to consider when planning an exam strategy

A tactical approach is important to ensure best use of limited time in the exam. Your answers to the questions below will help you frame a suitable strategy. You can usually find out these details from course handbooks or staff. Past papers are another source of information, but the rules may change, so confirm that the exam format is still the same.

1. How long is the exam?

2. How is the paper subdivided into sections and questions?

3. What is the nature of the questions/tasks, e.g. short/long answer responses or practical problems?

4. What proportion of the marks is allocated to each section/answer?

5. What restrictions on answering are there? How many questions/tasks must be answered/completed, and from which sections?

*Further points about effective exam strategy can be found in relevant chapters within **The Study Skills Book***

5.4 Checklist of items to take with you to each exam

It can help to reduce stress to know beforehand that you have everything you need ready for a forthcoming exam.

❏ Writing kit: pens and pencils (plus replacements); ruler; rubber; highlighter(s)

❏ Correction fluid (e.g. Tipp-Ex™), if allowed

❏ Student matriculation (ID) card (staff will use this to check your identity)

❏ Texts (for open book exams only)

❏ Clock or watch for time-keeping (you cannot use your mobile for this)

❏ Special equipment: calculators; protractor; compass; equipment for aural exams (check beforehand that you can use these aids properly); spare batteries

❏ Dictionary, if allowed, i.e. arranged beforehand with your department

❏ Sweets and a drink, if allowed

❏ Mascot

*Further points about preparing for exams and combating exam nerves can be found in relevant chapters within **The Study Skills Book***

5.5 Smart ways to improve your exam results

This list has been compiled using lecturers' opinions about why students perform poorly. When reading the list, think about your past exam performances and feedback from staff; decide whether attention to certain of the points might have helped you do better. What practical steps might you take to modify your approach to achieve greater success?

1. Ensure you answer/complete the exact questions/tasks as set.

2. Make sure you are equipped to recognise the specialist terms used in each question/task instruction.

3. Carry out the precise instruction in each question/task. (Sample instruction words are listed in **Planning Resource 2.6**).

4. Address all aspects of each question/task.

5. Focus on time management. Match the extent of your answer(s) to the time allocated. Do not spend too long on one question/task at the expense of the others.

6. Weight parts of each answer appropriately – recognise when one aspect (perhaps involving more complex ideas) may carry more marks than another.

7. Provide evidence to support your answers. Make sure you 'state the obvious' – give basic facts, cases, quotes or definitions.

8. Where appropriate, illustrate your answers by including a relevant diagram that aids communication.

9. Make sure your answers are neither incomplete nor shallow. Demonstrate your knowledge and understanding and make sure the topic is considered in sufficient depth.

10. Make sure all the evidence you cite is relevant. Never 'waffle' simply to fill space.

11. Make sure your handwriting is legible. If it can't be read, it can't be marked.

12. Write in good English, so that facts and ideas are expressed clearly.

13. Ensure there is an evident logic or structure to your answers.

14. Make sure your facts are correct.

15. Ensure you leave time to review your answers and correct any obvious errors.

Further points about revision and exam-sitting can be found in relevant chapters within
The Study Skills Book

6.1 Smart tips for effective personal development planning

The aim of personal development planning (PDP) is to help you to reflect on your progress as a student. PDP schemes (or similar) exist in most universities. The following tips will help you get the most out of the system in operation at your institution.

1. Be prepared to be reflective and self-critical about your talents, skills and achievements; recognise your strengths and consider areas you need to develop.

2. Visit a university careers adviser at an early stage, so you can find out and evaluate your career (and hence study) options. If you don't yet know what you want to do after university, this is even more reason to speak to a sympathetic expert, who will have a range of approaches to help you reach a decision.

3. Keep your CV up to date.

4. Consider the evidence you might be able to quote to substantiate any claims you may make about your skills and achievements. Keep computer and paper files of this material up to date.

5. Take responsibility for your own development by setting yourself personal and academic targets and evaluating progress towards these.

*Further points about PDP activities and career planning can be found in relevant chapters within **The Study Skills Book***

6.2 Self-audit tool for transferable skills

This table has been designed to help you appraise your skills as part of PDP or when preparing a CV. Rate each skill appropriately (see below for suggested scale), then make notes about those that you think you could or should develop further while at university (e.g. through specific coursework exercises, extra-curricular activities, part-time employment), and how you might be able to do this. Note: in this context, ICT means Information and Communications Technology.

Rating scale for your skills (circle or shade as appropriate):

1 point: Pretty basic level, as might be expected of a reasonably good school leaver

2 points: Accomplished in some aspects of the skill, with some relevant examples and/or experience

3 points: Good for most aspects of the skill, with extremely relevant examples and/or experience in most cases

4 points: All that could be expected of a graduate in your discipline, and possibly more

Skill category	Rating of skill level				How I could develop this skill
Analysing problems and tasks	1	2	3	4	
Career and entrepreneurial skills	1	2	3	4	
Communicating in a foreign language	1	2	3	4	
Contributing in meetings	1	2	3	4	
Critical thinking	1	2	3	4	
Cross-cultural awareness	1	2	3	4	
Dealing with data	1	2	3	4	
Designing experiments/surveys	1	2	3	4	
Discussing and debating	1	2	3	4	
Exam-sitting	1	2	3	4	

continued

Skill category	Rating of skill level				How I could develop this skill
Financial management	1	2	3	4	
ICT – general computing skills	1	2	3	4	
ICT – PowerPoint	1	2	3	4	
ICT – spreadsheets	1	2	3	4	
ICT – using the Web	1	2	3	4	
ICT – word-processing	1	2	3	4	
Information analysis	1	2	3	4	
Laboratory, studio or workplace skills	1	2	3	4	
Logical approach to problems	1	2	3	4	
Negotiating skills	1	2	3	4	
Note-making from texts	1	2	3	4	
Note-taking in lectures	1	2	3	4	
Numeracy – general arithmetic and maths	1	2	3	4	
Numeracy – specific maths skills	1	2	3	4	
Numeracy – statistics	1	2	3	4	
Performing under assessment	1	2	3	4	
Performing under stress	1	2	3	4	
Planning your work	1	2	3	4	
Preparing a poster	1	2	3	4	

Skill category	Rating of skill level				How I could develop this skill
Project management	1	2	3	4	
Reading for research purposes	1	2	3	4	
Report writing	1	2	3	4	
Social skills	1	2	3	4	
Speaking in public	1	2	3	4	
Study and revision skills	1	2	3	4	
Teamwork	1	2	3	4	
Thesis or dissertation writing	1	2	3	4	
Time-management	1	2	3	4	
Using library resources	1	2	3	4	
Writing – citing sources	1	2	3	4	
Writing essays and reports	1	2	3	4	
Writing letters, memos and emails	1	2	3	4	
Writing – organising and presenting	1	2	3	4	
Writing – use of English	1	2	3	4	
Other (specify)	1	2	3	4	
	1	2	3	4	
	1	2	3	4	

6.3 Summarising and organising your personal development planning activities

This table is one way of organising your thoughts and plans and it may assist you to reflect on your ambitions, character and skills in the context of your university's PDP scheme.

Aspect	Possible development points	Target dates	Achieved
Long-term aspirations and goals			
Medium-term aspirations and goals			
Short-term aspirations and goals			
Key interests and motivations			
Important personality and personal traits			
Transferable skills: strengths and areas for development			
Preferred learning style			

Date completed: _____

6.4 Elements of a typical CV

Maintaining a general CV (possibly as part of personal development planning) is a good idea. However, bear in mind that you should create a tailored application letter and CV for each job application.

Element, with alternatives	Usual contents
1. Personal details *Name and contact details*	Your full name, date of birth, contact address(es), contact phone numbers and email address(es).
2. Profile *Career aim; Career objective; Personal profile*	A summary of your career plans. Aspects of your intended goals and aspirations on which you would like the employer to focus.
3. Education *Qualifications; Education and qualifications*	Qualifications, including those that may be pending. Most people put their most recent qualifications first, then work backwards. Note educational institutions, years of attendance and the year each qualification or set of qualifications was gained. If relevant, give aspects of a subject covered in courses.
4. Work experience *Employment*	Details of past and current work (both paid and voluntary). Give dates, employer's name and job title. Add major duties if these are not obvious from the job title. List in reverse time sequence from present to past.
5. Skills and personal qualities *Skills and achievements; Skills and competences*	An indication of the match between your abilities and the job description. You may wish to refer to examples and evidence here.
6. Interests and activities *Interests; Leisure activities*	A chance to show your character, and present yourself as an interesting and enthusiastic colleague, e.g. sporting or volunteering activities that indicate you are a good team member. Employers will use this section to build a picture of you as a person; however, they may be put off someone who appears quirky or bizarre in their eyes. If this section is over-emphasised, they may assume that you have placed greater emphasis on your social life than on your studies.
7. Referees *References*	Where you provide the names and contact details for those who have agreed to provide a reference for you.

*Further points about writing your curriculum vitae (CV) can be found in relevant chapters within **The Study Skills Book***

7.1 Simplified rules of punctuation

Correct punctuation is vital for meaning and for getting your points across effectively. This table provides a reminder of the purpose of the main punctuation marks and lists examples of their use. Your tutors may use some of these terms in providing you with an explanation of an error.

Punctuation	Mark	How the mark is used
Apostrophe	'	• For possession, e.g. Napoleon's armies (singular owner); Students' essays (plural owner). • For contraction, e.g. Don't cry; I'm hungry; it's late. Note: *As its central theme, the book considered wind power* (no apostrophe required at **its**).
Brackets (parenthesis)	[. . .] (. . .)	• Square brackets [. . .]: for adding words within a quote. • Round brackets (. . .): information to isolate explanatory information.
Capital letter	ABC	• Starts sentences, proper nouns, seasons, rivers, mountain ranges, places, Acts of Parliament, titles, organisations, e.g. the **U**nited **N**ations.
Colon	:	• Divides two ideas framed as sentences but joined by a colon, where the second sentence explains the first more fully, e.g. I hate travelling by plane: the waiting time is usually long and delays are frequent. • Introduces lists. • Introduces a 'long quote'.
Comma	. . . ,	• Separates items in a list of three or more, e.g. tea, beer, juice and wine. • Separates part of a sentence, e.g. He came home, ate and fell asleep. • Separates additional information within a sentence, e.g. Rugby, in the main, is a contact sport. • Marks adverbs and signpost words, e.g. Certainly, the results have been positive.
Dash	–	• Marks an aside/addition, e.g. Murder – regardless of reason – is a crime.

Punctuation	Mark	How the mark is used
Ellipsis	. . .	• Marks words omitted from a quotation, e.g. 'taxes . . . mean price rises'.
Exclamation mark	!	• Shows shock, horror, e.g. Help! Exclamation marks are rarely used in academic writing.
Full stop (period)	.	• Marks the end of a sentence, e.g. This is the end. • Marks an abbreviation, e.g., etc., i.e., p.a.
Hyphen	-	• Joins a single letter to an existing word, e.g. x-ray. • Separates prefixes, e.g. post-modern. • Prevents repetition of certain letters, e.g. semi-independent. • Joins a prefix to a proper noun, e.g. pro-British. • Creates a noun from a phrasal verb, e.g. show-off. • Joins numbers and fractions, e.g. Twenty-three; three-quarters. • Used to split longer words that are too long for a line. The hyphen is placed between syllables, e.g. imita-tion.
Italics	*Italics*	• Differentiates text to show quotations, titles of publications in citations, species, works of art, foreign words, e.g. *déjà vu*; *et al.*
Question mark	?	• Ends sentences asking a direct question, e.g. Where?
Quotation marks (inverted commas)	'. . .' ". . ."	• 'Single quotation marks' mark exact words spoken/ printed in a text. • "Double quotation marks" place a quotation within a quotation (British English). • Note that in some word-processing packages it is possible to choose between slanted 'smart quotes' (". . . ") and 'straight quotes' (". . . ").
Semi-colon	;	• Separates two or more sentences of equal importance and closely related in meaning, e.g. They won the battle; the other side won the war. • Separates listed items, especially when the description of each item uses several words.

7.2 Basic spelling rules

Spelling is tricky for many students. In English, the 'rules' are difficult to define because often there are exceptions to them. Here are some of the fundamental rules with some examples of exceptions where these occur. Creating a personal glossary can help you learn to spell the jargon and technical words of your discipline.

Number	Rule	Examples with exceptions as applicable
Rule 1	**'ie' and 'ei' confusion**	
1.1	'i' comes before 'e' (except after 'c')	belief, relief, chief *but* receive, perceive, deceive, ceiling
Rule 2	**Verbs**	
2.1	where verbs end in -eed and -ede, then the -eed ending goes with succ-/exc-/proc-; -ede applies in all other cases	-eed: succeed, exceed, proceed -ede: precede, concede
2.2	where verbs end with -ise, nouns end with -ice	practise (verb)/practice (noun) *but* exercise: verb and noun
Rule 3	**Double letters**	
3.1	Double final consonants before using -ing, -ed, -er or -est when the words are single syllable and end with b/d/g/m/n/p/r/t	robbed, ridding, bagging, summing, running, hopper, furred, fittest
3.2	Double consonant when the stressed syllable is at the end of the word	occurred, beginning, forgettable
3.3	Double 'l' when words end in an 'l' preceded by a short vowel	travelled, levelled
Rule 4	**Adjectives from nouns**	
4.1	Nouns ending in '-our', drop the 'u' in the adjective form	glamour, glamorous; humour, humorous

Number	Rule	Examples with exceptions as applicable
Rule 5	**Plurals**	
5.1	generally add '-s'; or '-es' if after ss/x/ch/sh	boys, cats, dogs; crosses, fixes, churches, dishes
5.2	Nouns ending in -y drop -y and add -ies	ally/allies; copy/copies *but* monkeys; donkeys
5.3	Nouns ending in -o, then add -s for the plural	photos; pianos *but* tomatoes; volcanoes; heroes
5.4	Nouns ending in -f and -fe, no consistent rule.	chief/chiefs *but* half/halves
5.5	Some 'foreign' nouns follow the rules of their own language in the plural	medium/media; criterion/criteria; datum/data; phenomenon/phenomena (shown in singular/plural order)
5.6	Hyphenated words in the plural	brothers-in-law; commanders-in-chief
5.7	Some nouns are the same format for singular and for plural	sheep, fish
Rule 6	**Prefixes**	
6.1	dis- and mis- do not add extra letters	dis+agree, mis+manage, *but* note dis+satisfaction/dissatisfaction
6.2	double 'l' becomes single 'l' in compounds	full + fill = fulfil; hope + full = hopeful
Rule 7	**Suffixes**	
7.1	-ful, -fully, -al, -ally: adjectives formed with the suffix 'ful' and 'al' have only one 'l'	careful; hopeful *but* adverbs add -ly: carefully and hopefully
7.2	When forming adverbs, add -ly	skilfully, marginally
7.3	Adjectives ending in -ic form their adverbs with -ally	basic/basically *but* public/publicly
7.4	Silent 'e' usually keep -e when adding the suffix	hope + full = hopeful

continued

Number	Rule	Examples with exceptions as applicable
7.5	If suffix begins with a vowel, then drop final -e	come + ing = coming
7.6	After words ending in -ce or -ge, keep -e to keep sounds soft	noticeable, courageous
7.7	For words ending in -y that are preceded by a consonant, change -y to -i before any suffix except -ing, -ist, -ish	dry/driest *but* drying, copyist, dryish
7.8	For joins within word, do not add or subtract letters at 'join'	meanness
Rule 8	**Silent letters**	
8.1	The letters b; g; k; l; p; w are not pronounced in certain words	de**b**t, **g**nat, **k**not, ta**l**k, **p**sychiatrist, **w**rong
Rule 9	**Latin words in English**	
9.1	ending in -ex or -ix in the singular, end in -ices in the plural	index, indices; appendix, appendices
9.2	ending in -um in the singular, end in -a in the plural	datum, data; medium, media; stratum, strata
9.3	ending -us in the singular, end in -ii in the plural	radius, radii
9.4	ending in -a in the singular, end in -ae in the plural	agenda, agendae; formula, formulae
Rule 10	**Greek words in English**	
10.1	ending in -ion in the singular, end in -ia in the plural	criterion, criteria
10.2	ending in -sis in the singular, end in -ses in the plural	analysis, analyses; hypothesis, hypotheses

Further points about improving spelling can be found in relevant chapters within **The Study Skills Book**

7.3 Definitions of grammatical terms

This table revisits the language of grammar as an aid to understanding comments about grammar errors in written feedback from tutors on your script. Similarly, it may be of assistance in helping you to understand and follow the directions provided by your grammar-checking software. If you have only a basic knowledge of grammar and would like to learn more, then it may be helpful to seek more information from an appropriate grammar text (e.g. Stott, R. and Chapman, P. (2001) *Grammar and Writing,* Longman, Harlow).

Grammar term	Explanation	Example
adjective	Describes nouns or gerunds (e.g. things, actions or concepts).	A **red** book; an **innovative** project; **diligent** researching.
adverb	Adds information as to how something is done.	The student read **quickly**.
articles	There are only three in English: a, an, the. There are particular rules about using them and you will find these in a grammar book.	**A** shot in the dark; **an** empty house; **the** Highway Code.
clause	Part of sentence containing a verb. If the verb and the words relating to it can stand alone, then they comprise the main clause. If the words cannot stand alone, then the verb and the words that go with it form a subordinate clause.	Cats eat mice **which are vermin**. [main clause] + [**subordinate clause**].
conditional	Used to explain future possible situation, note the comma after the condition.	**If I had the time**, I would go out. [**condition**] [consequence]
conjunction	Word that joins two clauses in a sentence where the ideas are connected or equally balanced.	The book was on loan **and** the student had to reserve it.
demonstratives	There are four in English: **this, these, that, those**.	**This** house supports the abolition of smoking in public.

continued

Grammar term	Explanation	Example
direct object	The noun or pronoun which is affected by the verb.	Foxes kill **sheep**. Foxes eat **them**.
future tense	Presenting things that have not yet happened. Use 'will' or 'shall' for predictions, willingness, offers, promises; use 'going to' for plans and intentions.	I **shall** work until I am sixty-five. They **will** come early. He is **going to** work harder.
gerunds	The gerund acts as a noun and is formed with the part of the verb called the present participle: . . . -ing.	**Speaking** is easier than **writing** for most people. I **will** teach you to drive. I **will** pay your fees for the next year.
indirect object	The person or thing that benefits from the action of a verb.	Tutors give (to) **students** written work. They give (to) **them** essays.
infinitive	Sometimes called the simple or root form of the verb. This form is usually listed in dictionaries, but without 'to'.	e.g. **to work**.
nouns	Term used to refer to things or people; e.g. abstract (non-visible), concrete (visible) and proper nouns (names of people, places, organisations, rivers, mountain ranges).	**Abstract nouns:** thought. **Concrete nouns:** chair, table. **Proper nouns:** Caesar, Rome, the Post Office, the Rhine, the Andes.
passive voice	Used to describe things objectively, that is, placing the emphasis of the sentence on the action rather than the actor. Although some electronic grammar checkers imply that the passive is wrong, it is perfectly correct and is often used in academic writing.	**Essays are written** by students. [action] [actor]
past participle	Usually formed by adding -ed to the verb stem, but in English there are many irregular verbs. You will find lists of these verbs in some dictionaries.	Work**ed** BUT many irregular verbs, e.g. **bent, done, drunk, eaten, gone, seen, thought, understood**.

Grammar term	Explanation	Example
phrasal verbs	These verbs have a particle or particles (see prepositions) as one of their components. These verbs are generally regarded as being less formal in tone than single word verbs.	**Set down** (deposit), **pick up** (collect), **write down** (note), **look out for** (observe).
possessives	Words indicating ownership: my, mine, your, yours, his, her, its, our, ours, their, theirs.	**My** house and **his** are worth the same. **Mine** is larger but **his** has more land.
prepositions	Words used with nouns. Sometimes these are followed by an article, sometimes not, e.g. at, by, in, for, from, of, on, over, through, under, with.	Put money **in** the bank **for** a rainy day or save it **for** summer holidays **in** the sun.
present participle	This is formed by adding -ing to the simple verb form (sometimes involving spelling adjustments). It is used to form continuous verb tenses.	The sun is **setting**. We were **watching** the yachts.
pronouns	Words used instead of nouns: I, me, you, he, him, she, her, it, we, us, they, them. Also words such as one, each, everyone.	I have given **it** to **him**. **We** gave **them** information for **him**.
relative pronouns	Words that link adjective clauses to the noun about which they give more information: that, which, who, whose, whom.	This is the house **that** Jack built. Jack, **who** owns it, lives there. Jack, **whose** wife sings, is a baker. Jack, to **whom** we sold the flour, used it.
sentence	The smallest grouping of words, one of which must be a verb, which can stand together independently and make sense.	**The people elect their leaders in a democracy**.
subject	The person or thing that performs the action in a sentence.	**Caesar** invaded Britain. **Caterpillars** eat leaves.

continued

Grammar term	Explanation	Example
tense	In English, to show past, present and future tense shifts, the verb changes. This often involves adding a word to show this. Some verbs behave irregularly from the standard rules. Here are three basic tenses; more can be found in a grammar book or language learner's dictionary.	**Simple Past** I studied | we studied you studied | you studied s/he studied | they studied **Present** I study | we study you study | you study s/he studies | they study **Future** I will study | we will study you will study | you will study s/he will study | they will study
topic introducer (TI)/topic sentence (TS)	The first sentence in a paragraph introduces the key point of the text; the topic (second) sentence explains the paragraph content.	**Skiing is a popular sport. (TI) Skiers enjoy this in winter on real snow and in summer on dry slopes. (TS)**
verb	The action or 'doing' word in a sentence. It changes form to indicate shifts in time (see tense) and who is 'doing' the action (I, you, he/she/it, we, you [plural], they).	**I work, I am working, I will work, I worked, I was working, I have worked, I had worked.**

7.4 How to resolve common errors in grammar

This table lists the more common errors in grammar that often occur in student writing. It provides examples of the typical error and offers correct models for comparison.

Error	Incorrect examples (✗) and correction (✓)
1. Comparing Sometimes there is confusion with when to use a word ending in -er or -est rather than using more or most. For grammar book entry, look for **Comparatives** and **Superlatives**	Comparing two things: ✗ The debit was more bigger than the credit. ✓ The debit was **greater** than the credit. Comparing three or more things: ✗ China has the most greatest population in the world. ✓ China has the **greatest** population in the world. Countable and non-countable: ✗ Cars are more safer than motorbikes. ✓ Cars are safer than motorbikes. ✗ Flowers are beautifulest in summer. ✓ Flowers are most beautiful in summer. Irregular comparisons (exceptions to the 'rule'): ✗ Weather is bad in autumn, but more bad in winter. ✓ Weather is bad in autumn, but worse in winter. ✗ Frost is most worse in winter. ✓ Frost is worst in winter.
2. Describing Commas are vital to meaning where a 'wh-' clause is used. For grammar book entry, look for **Relative clauses**	✗ Toys, which are dangerous, should not be given to small children. ✓ Toys which are dangerous should not be given to small children.
3. Encapsulating Using one word to represent a previous word or idea. For grammar book entry, look for **Demonstrative pronoun**	✗ . . . impact of diesel use on air quality. This increases in rush-hour. ✓ . . . impact of diesel use on air quality. **This impact** increases in rush-hour, **OR** ✓ . . . impact of diesel use on air quality. **This use** increases in rush-hour, **OR** ✓ . . . impact of diesel use on air quality. **This air quality** increases in rush-hour. (unlikely) (Be sure that what 'this' or 'these', 'that' or 'those' represents is identifiable in the previous sentence.)

continued

Error	Incorrect examples (✗) and correction (✓)
4. Its/it's These two terms are often confused. For grammar book entry, look for **Possessives** (its) and **Apostrophes** (it's)	✗ As it's aim, the book describes the whole problem. ✓ As **its** aim, the book describes the whole problem. (possession) ✗ Its not a viable answer to the problem. ✓ **It's** not a viable answer to the problem. (It is . . .) ✗ Its not had a good review. ✓ **It's** not had a good review. (It has . . .)
5. Joining Words such as 'because', 'but' and 'and' join two clauses; they should not be used to begin sentences. For grammar book entry, look for **Conjunctions**	✗ Because the sample was too small, the results were invalid. ✓ The results were invalid **because** the sample was too small. ('Because' is a conjunction and is used to join two ideas.) ✗ But the UN failed to act. And the member states did nothing. ✓ The country was attacked, **but** the UN failed to act **and** the member states did nothing. ('but' and 'and' are conjunctions that join two separate ideas)
6. Double negative Two negatives mean a positive. Sometimes using a double negative can cause confusion. For grammar book entry, look for **Double negatives**	✗ They have not had no results from their experiments. ✓ They have not had **any** results from their experiments. ✗ The government had not done nothing to alleviate poverty. ✓ The government had done **nothing** to alleviate poverty.
7. Past participles These are sometimes misused, especially when the verbs are irregular. For grammar book entry, look for **Past participles**	✗ The team had went to present their findings. ✓ The team had **gone** to present their findings. ✗ The lecturer has did this before. ✓ The lecturer has **done** this before.
8. Preposition These should not come at the end of a sentence. For grammar book entry, look for **Prepositions**	✗ These figures are the ones you will work with. ✓ These figures are the ones **with which** you will work.

Error	Incorrect examples (✗) and correction (✓)
9. Pronouns These are used to replace nouns. The singular pronouns often cause confusion because they need to agree with the verb. For grammar book entry, look for **Pronouns**	**Singular pronouns** – anybody, anyone, anything, each, either, everybody, everyone, everything, neither, nobody, no-one, nothing, somebody, someone, something take a singular verb. ✗ Each of the new measures are to be introduced separately. ✓ Each of the new measures **is** to be introduced separately. **Reflexive pronouns** ✗ They only have theirselves to blame. ✓ They only have **themselves** to blame.
10. Quantifiers Words that are used to refer to countable items, e.g. things counted individually and non-countable items, e.g. salt, oil, coal (cannot be counted as individual items). For grammar book entry, look for **Quantifiers**	**Fewer/less** ✗ This queue is for 10 purchases or less. ✓ This queue is for 10 purchases or fewer. 'fewer' for countable items; 'less' for non-countable items. **Amount/number** ✗ A greater amount of falls occur in the home. ✓ A greater number of falls occur in the home. 'falls' are countable, thus 'number of' is correct.
11. Subject–verb agreement Often singular subjects are matched with plural verbs and vice versa. For grammar book entry, look for **Subject–verb agreement**	✗ The Principal, together with the Chancellor, were present. ✓ The Principal, together with the Chancellor, **was** present. ✗ It is the result of these overtures and influences that help to mould personal identity. ✓ It is the **result** of these overtures and influences that **helps** to mould personal identity.
12. There/Their/They're These simply need to be remembered. For grammar book entry, look for **Words that are often confused** or **Homophones**. Note 'they're' is a contraction of 'they are'. Contractions are not usually used in academic writing.	✗ They finished there work before noon. ✓ **They** finished **their** work before noon. ✗ We have six places at the conference. We'll go their. ✓ We have six places **at the conference**. We'll go **there**. ✗ Researchers are skilled but there not highly paid. ✓ **Researchers** are skilled but **they're** not highly paid.

*Further points about improving grammar can be found in relevant chapters within **The Study Skills Book***

7.5 Examples of a standard graph and table

Disciplines have codes for the ways in which graphic and tabular information are presented. The following images illustrate common features of graphs and tables that can be used as models in many cases. If in doubt about any aspect of presentation, refer to guidance supplied by your department in course handbooks.

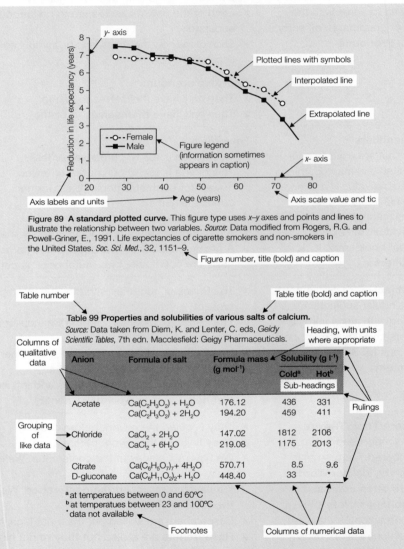

Figure 89 A standard plotted curve. This figure type uses x–y axes and points and lines to illustrate the relationship between two variables. *Source*: Data modified from Rogers, R.G. and Powell-Griner, E., 1991. Life expectancies of cigarette smokers and non-smokers in the United States. *Soc. Sci. Med.*, 32, 1151–9.

Table number

Table title (bold) and caption

Table 99 Properties and solubilities of various salts of calcium.
Source: Data taken from Diem, K. and Lenter, C. eds, *Geidy Scientific Tables*, 7th edn. Macclesfield: Geigy Pharmaceuticals.

Heading, with units where appropriate

Columns of qualitative data

Grouping of like data

Anion	Formula of salt	Formula mass (g mol^{-1})	Solubility (g l^{-1})	
			Cold[a]	Hot[b]
Acetate	$Ca(C_2H_3O_2) + H_2O$	176.12	436	331
	$Ca(C_2H_3O_2) + 2H_2O$	194.20	459	411
Chloride	$CaCl_2 + 2H_2O$	147.02	1812	2106
	$CaCl_2 + 6H_2O$	219.08	1175	2013
Citrate	$Ca(C_6H_5O_7)_7 + 4H_2O$	570.71	8.5	9.6
D-gluconate	$Ca(C_6H_{11}O_2)_2 + H_2O$	448.40	33	*

Sub-headings

Rulings

[a] at temperatues between 0 and 60°C
[b] at temperatues between 23 and 100°C
* data not available

Footnotes

Columns of numerical data

Further points about laying out graphs and tables, and interpreting and presenting data can be found in relevant chapters within **The Study Skills Book**

7.6 Standard geometric formulae

These equations can be used to calculate or estimate the perimeter, area or volume of different shapes and objects.

Shape and diagram	Perimeter (2D objects)	Area (2D objects) or surface area (3D objects)	Volume (3D objects)
Square	$4x$	x^2	
Cube		$6x^2$	x^3
Rectangle	$2(x + y)$	xy	
Cuboid		$2xy + 2xz + 2yx$	xyz
Circle	$2\pi r$	πr^2	
Sphere		$4\pi r^2$	$4\pi r^3/3$
Cylinder		$2\pi rh + 2\pi r^2$	$\pi r^2 h$
Ellipse	$\pi[(1.5a + b) - \sqrt{ab}]$ (approximation)	πab	
Ellipsoid		No simple formula	$\pi(abc)/3$
Triangle	$x + y + z$	$zh/2$	
Cone		$ph/2 + b$, where $p = 2\pi r$ and $b = \pi r^2$	$bh/3$
Pyramid		$ph/2 + b$, where $p = 4x$ and $b = x^2$	$bh/3$

Key: x, y, z = sides; a, b, c = axes; r = radius, h = height or perpendicular height; p = perimeter of base; b = area of base (cone and pyramid).

*Further points about numeracy can be found in relevant chapters within **The Study Skills Book***

7.7 SI units and prefixes

The *Système International d'Unités* (SI) is used in most scientific disciplines to aid communication and understanding of numerical data. Each value has a number and a unit, and prefixes are used immediately before units (no space) to describe small or large values.

Quantity	SI unit (and symbol)
Base units	
Length	metre (m)
Mass	kilogramme (kg)
Time	second (s)
Temperature	kelvin (K)
Amount of substance	mole (mol)
Electric current	ampere (A)
Luminous intensity	candela (cd)
Supplementary units	
Plane angle	radian (rad)
Solid angle	steradian (sr)

Some examples of compound units	
Energy	joule (J) = m^2 kg s^{-2} = N m
Force	newton (N) = m kg s^{-2} = J m^{-1}
Pressure	pascal (Pa) = kg m^{-1} s^{-2} = N m^{-2}
Power	watt (W) = m^2 kg s^{-3} = J s^{-1}
Electric charge	coulomb (C) = A s
Illumination	lux (lx) = cd sr m^{-2}

Prefixes for small numbers		
Value	Prefix	Symbol
10^{-3}	milli	m
10^{-6}	micro	μ
10^{-9}	nano	n
10^{-12}	pico	p
10^{-15}	femto	f
10^{-18}	atto	a
10^{-21}	zepto	z
10^{-24}	yocto	y

Prefixes for large numbers		
Value	Prefix	Symbol
10^3	kilo	k
10^6	mega	M
10^9	giga	G
10^{12}	tera	T
10^{15}	peta	P
10^{18}	exa	E
10^{21}	zeta	Z
10^{24}	yotta	Y

7.8 Smart tips for delivering spoken presentations

A good presentation requires careful planning and organisation. Knowing that your material has been well prepared is also a way of reducing any nerves you may have. By working through the following list, you can ensure you raise your confidence and avoid basic errors.

Basic aspects to consider when preparing a talk

→ Audience – will they be experts, your peers, lay people or a mixture?

→ Arrangements – what is the date, start time and period allocated for your talk?

→ Venue – how might the location and nature of its layout affect your delivery?

→ Facilities – what equipment and audio-visual (AV) aids will be available?

→ Context – who will be preceding and/or following you?

→ Presentation style – do you want to use 'chalk and talk', overhead transparencies or slide delivery system such as PowerPoint? Will you use a detailed script, prompts or simply improvise?

→ Requirements – what might you need to bring? Which equipment might you need to practise with beforehand?

→ Liaison – who should you contact to confirm details or make special requests?

Structuring your talk

→ Keep it simple: 'say what you are going to say, say it, then say what you've said'

→ Start your talk with the basics, such as definitions of key terms

→ Keep your introduction positive and your conclusions simple and clear

Effective presentation

→ Dress appropriately for the occasion

→ Make sure you can be heard – ask the audience

→ Make sure your audio-visual aids can be seen

→ Engage the audience. Be sensitive to their body language.

→ Try to enjoy the occasion. To reduce your tension, take deep breaths

→ Don't speak too quickly – pace your talk

→ Anticipate likely questions and prepare responses

Practice makes perfect

→ Go through your talk beforehand to help you become more confident

→ Practise difficult or complex parts of the talk independently

→ Check whether your talk will fit the allotted time

→ Ask a friend to comment on your audibility and presentation style

Further points about spoken presentations can be found in relevant chapters within ***The Study Skills Book***

7.9 Smart tips for planning and presenting posters

Posters are used increasingly in university assessments, yet many students are unfamiliar with this as a medium for communicating their work. The aim of a poster is to 'advertise' the research you have done in a clear, easily assimilated presentation. These tips should help you to plan and organise, present and defend a display.

Typical components of a poster

→ Title

→ Author information (names, and in the formal academic type of poster, their affiliation and contact information)

→ Abstract or summary, stating the approach taken and the main conclusions

→ Introduction

→ Materials and methods, and, if describing experimental or field research, background theory or historical overview

→ Results, key findings or examples

→ Conclusions

→ Acknowledgements, stating who has helped you

→ Corporate logo, if appropriate

Planning and organising

→ Learn from good and bad aspects of research posters in your department

→ Find out the dimensions of your poster space and draw this out to scale

→ Map out your poster before constructing it at full size (see figure)

→ Ensure your poster is able to 'travel well' from point of construction to point of presentation

Presentational aspects

→ Use the poster title effectively

→ Use language (e.g. rhetorical questions) to draw the reader in

→ Check out the font sizes you plan to use – should be readable at 1.5 metres

→ Remember that 'white space' is important in design

→ Use imaginative materials

→ Consider colour combinations carefully

→ Follow any prescribed restrictions as to size and layout

The poster content

→ Don't provide too much written detail

→ State your take-home message clearly

→ Use a handout if you have too much detail to cover

Defending your poster

→ Hold a mock presentation with a flatmate or friend

→ Be ready to answer the following questions about your poster. Why did you select this topic? Who did which part of the research? Who thought of the design? Who made up the components? Can you give me further information on . . . ? How does this finding relate to . . . ? What does this graph or image mean? Where next for this topic or research area? How might you improve your poster?

Options for laying out a poster. The numbers and arrows indicate the reading sequence to be followed, while the shaded bar at the top would contain the title and author details.

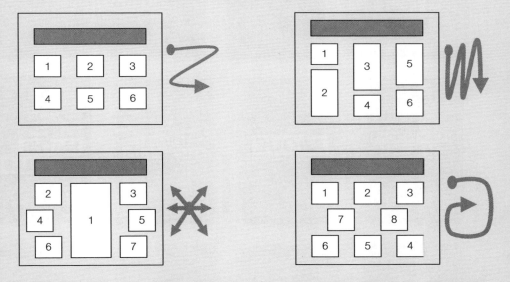

Further points about presenting posters can be found in relevant chapters within **The Study Skills Book**

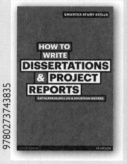

Your university course

Keep a note of your module details in the table below as you'll need to quote these for university administration purposes.

Semester	Module code	Module title

Additional notes about your course and modules

9 Semester/term planner and timetable templates

Semester/term _____

🕐	Monday	Tuesday	Wednesday	Thursday	Friday
08:00					
08:30					
09:00					
09:30					
10:00					
10:30					
11:00					
11:30					
12:00					
12:30					
13:00					
13:30					
14:00					
14:30					
15:00					
15:30					
16:00					
16:30					
17:00					
17:30					
18:00					
18:30					
Evening					

Semester/term planner and timetable templates

Semester/term _____

🕐	Monday	Tuesday	Wednesday	Thursday	Friday
08:00					
08:30					
09:00					
09:30					
10:00					
10:30					
11:00					
11:30					
12:00					
12:30					
13:00					
13:30					
14:00					
14:30					
15:00					
15:30					
16:00					
16:30					
17:00					
17:30					
18:00					
18:30					
Evening					

Semester/term planner and timetable templates

Semester/term ____

⏰	Monday	Tuesday	Wednesday	Thursday	Friday
08:00					
08:30					
09:00					
09:30					
10:00					
10:30					
11:00					
11:30					
12:00					
12:30					
13:00					
13:30					
14:00					
14:30					
15:00					
15:30					
16:00					
16:30					
17:00					
17:30					
18:00					
18:30					